Of Bread and Circuses

The Story of Bountygate and the 2012 New Orleans Saints

By Reid Gilbert

***

Copyright 2013, Reid Gilbert

All Rights Reserved

This book and its author are not affiliated with the New Orleans Saints or the NFL.

table of contents

[1] **Introduction**

[3] **Chapter 1** A Defensive Makeover

[7] **Chapter 2** March 2, 2012: The Arrival of Bountygate

[14] **Chapter 3** The Football World Reacts

[21] **Chapter 4** Saints' Coaches, Organization Punished

[30] **Chapter 5** The Brees' Negotiations

[33] **Chapter 6** The Parcells' Flirtation

[38] **Chapter 7** "Kill the Head"

[44] **Chapter 8** The Wiretapping Allegations

[49] **Chapter 9** Conduct Detrimental

[59] **Chapter 10** Challenging the Franchise Tag Designation

[63] **Chapter 11** Examining the Bountygate Evidence

[83] **Chapter 12** "Pure Fantasy" – or – "What The Hell Are You Doing, Roger?"

[94] **Chapter 13** Mike Cerullo: The Disgruntled Whistleblower

[102] **Chapter 14** An Investigation and an Induction

[107] **Chapter 15** Holding Court

[118] **Chapter 16** Dueling Declarations

[130] **Chapter 17** A Historic Night

[134] **Chapter 18** "A Big Sham"

[145] **Chapter 19** A Recusal, a Revelation, and a Rivalry

[152] **Chapter 20** Peak and Valley

table of contents, continued

[156] **Chapter 21** The Tagliabue Ruling

[170] **Chapter 22** Looming Infamy

[173] **The Legacy of Bountygate**

* The NFL's Motives

* Roger Goodell's Credibility

* Why The Saints?

* A Final Word

[191] **Coda**: Sean Payton, A Second Act

"The phrase 'conduct detrimental to the league' could be interpreted in sweeping ways, and a lot of palace intrigue can be concealed behind the distractions of bread and circuses."

- *Mike Tanier,* Sports on Earth*, 13 September 2012*

"The public has long since cast off its cares; the people that once bestowed commands, consulships, legions and all else, now meddles no more and longs eagerly for just two things, bread and circuses."

- *Juvenal, 100 A.D.*

introduction

Sometimes, a strange fulfillment emerges from the unlikeliest of circumstances.

During the 2012 calendar year, the New Orleans Saints found themselves repeatedly battered by setbacks. After the Saints' mostly flawless, six-year run towards prominence and glory, much of the ubiquitous optimism and hope surrounding the team came crashing down in an unforeseeable flash.

Dismantled at the peak of their powers -- a level of performance nearly fifty years in the making -- the Saints and their fans were left to sort through the wreckage of both collapse and witch hunt for much of 2012.

Setting the stage for this sudden reversal of fortune was the Saints' shocking rebirth in 2006 and the team's first appearance in an NFC Championship Game that same season. A mere three seasons later, the Saints brought a Super Bowl trophy back to New Orleans and, with it, a bright hope for the future.

Two years later in 2011 the Saints fielded a team that perhaps eclipsed the talent level of the legendary 2009 team. The 2011 Saints set several seasonal NFL records: the Saints' offense, for yards gained; Drew Brees, for passing yards and completion percentage; and newly-acquired Darren Sproles, for all-purpose yards gained.

By the end of the 2011 regular season, the Saints had won eight consecutive games by an average margin of 17.1 points per game. After scoring 35 points in the second half of their wild card playoff game against the Detroit Lions, en route to winning 45-28, the Saints had scored 42, 45, 45, and 45 points in their then most recent four games.

In those four games, the Saints averaged an astounding 569.8 yards per game, including consecutive games of 600-plus yards, while beating their opponents by an obscene 24 points per game.

By all appearances, the Saints had reached the apex of their abilities under Sean Payton. They were certifiably unstoppable.

And then they weren't.

On Saturday January 14th, 2012, in a divisional playoff game versus the San Francisco 49ers -- a despised, longtime nemesis -- it all unraveled for the Saints.

The offense lost runningback Pierre Thomas to a concussion from a vicious helmet-to-helmet collision on the game's opening drive, compounding the absences of both Mark Ingram and Lance Moore. Hamstrung, the offense and special teams turned the ball over five times, a Payton-era high. The 13-3 49ers, owners of the NFL's best defense in 2011, jumped out to a 17-0 lead.

Almost miraculously, the Saints fought back to take the lead *twice* in the 4th quarter before finally losing the game with just nine seconds left. It was an unfathomably cruel, soul-crushing loss for a team and fanbase intent on and certain of another Super Bowl title.

As painful as that loss was, that was only the beginning of the trauma facing the Saints and their fans in 2012. Over the next eleven months, an unprecedented course of events would unfold and befall the Saints -- unthinkable, unjust, enraging, dispiriting, and rarely affirming.

For Saints' fans, the unlikely fulfillment provided by the battering of 2012 came in the form of a unique bond of fandom, of a season unlike any other in the history of the NFL, of a collective rage against the NFL machine. Today, the wounds remain.

This is the story of Bountygate and the 2012 New Orleans Saints.

1: a defensive makeover

Almost immediately after the Saints' playoff loss to San Francisco in mid-January, Saints' defensive coordinator Gregg Williams was on his way out of New Orleans for good.

Williams, who would soon become Bountygate's most nefarious figure, arrived in New Orleans in 2009 amid much fanfare. After the Saints' defense had slogged through three middling seasons under the direction of Gary Gibbs from 2006 – 2008, Sean Payton handpicked Gregg Williams to rebuild the Saints' defense.

Fans and pundits alike considered Williams the missing ingredient in a winning Super Bowl formula for the Saints.

By 2009 Gregg Williams had built an extensive, and mostly impressive, NFL resume.[1] From 1997 – 2000, Williams coached the Tennessee Titans' defense and, in 2000, led a unit ranked #1 in the league on the way to a Super Bowl appearance.

Williams parlayed his success in Tennessee into a head coaching job in Buffalo from 2001 – 2003. After three mostly nondescript years as the Bills' head coach, though one where he led his team to a stellar defensive season in 2003,[2] Williams moved on to the defensive coordinator role with the Washington Redskins under the direction of the legendary Joe Gibbs. There, Williams immediately transformed the Redskins' defense into one of the league's best units in just one season.[3]

After the (second) Joe Gibbs' era in Washington ended after the 2007 season, Williams moved on to Jacksonville in 2008 for one season as the team's defensive coordinator. There the Jaguars' defense failed to perform at anything other than a mediocre level, and speculation surfaced about "philosophical" differences[4] between Williams and Jacksonville head coach Jack del Rio. Perhaps due to del Rio's presence in defensive meetings and insistence on calling defensive plays,[5] Williams' days in Jacksonville were short-lived.

Following the 2008 season, Williams left Jacksonville and sought coaching employment elsewhere. A January 2009 report from nola.com indicated that Gregg Williams "expected to be one of the most sought-after and highly paid defensive coordinators"[6] for the upcoming 2009 season. The Saints' interest in Williams crested early in 2009 as both Green Bay and Houston vied for his services concurrently.

In what's now become a well-publicized anecdote, and possible cautionary tale, Saints' head coach Sean Payton almost single-handedly swayed Williams' decision in the Saints' favor. First reported by *FOX's* Jay Glazer,[7] Payton offered $250,000 of his own salary in order to land Williams for the 2009 season.

Pro Football Talk's Mike Florio further explained in a February 2010 report:[8]

> In January of 2009, Sean Payton coughed up a quarter of a million dollars so that the Saints could afford to hire his preferred choice of defensive coordinators, Gregg Williams. After winning Super Bowl XLIV, Payton joked in an appearance on NFL Network that he gave up the money under the influence, and woke up having second thoughts.
>
> "I had a few beers in me," Payton said. "Woke up the next morning, and my wife said, 'What?'"
>
> But on a serious note, Payton said that what it all boiled down to was, "It'd be a shame to lose a good coach over $250,000."
>
> Payton added, "I just wanted to make sure ownership, and the General Manager Mickey Loomis knew that this is who we needed."

With Williams in the fold for 2009, the Saints' defense finished second in the NFL in takeaways, a key factor that fueled the team's Super Bowl run. Additionally, Williams instilled in his defense a signature attacking mentality. Saints' defensive captain Jonathan Vilma referred to Gregg Williams as "cutthroat" and "no-nonsense."[9]

After the Super Bowl win in 2009 and a noticeable defensive improvement during the 2010 regular season,[10] the Gregg Williams' defense in New Orleans showed signs of fissure, starting with a defensive collapse against Seattle in a wildcard game during the 2010-'11 postseason.

In that game, the Saints allowed 41 points to one of the league's least-accomplished offenses (a 7-9 team) and ultimately fell short of defending their Super Bowl title.

A year later, those same shortcomings coalesced in the January playoff game versus the 49ers where Williams recklessly failed to protect the Saints' lead in the waning moments of the game.

Of Williams' decisions in that game, Mike Lombardi -- then of the *NFL Network*, now V.P. of Player Personnel with the Cleveland Browns -- explained in detail:[11]

> It was obvious to experts watching the contest that Williams was more interested in showcasing his play-calling skills in front of a large television audience than doing what was needed to win the game.
>
> The most destructive element on any staff is when a coach allows his ego -- or his personal ambition -- to get in the way of winning. It's a team game. Doing what is needed to win will make everyone shine, while seeking personal glory can prevent winning.

Just a day after the loss in San Francisco, reports surfaced that Gregg Williams would be departing the Saints' organization.[12] The team allowed Williams' contract to expire, did not seek to re-sign him,[13] and speculation mounted that a gulf had emerged between Payton and Williams. *Yahoo's!* Mike Silver reported that Williams "had been essentially fired by Sean Payton, who sought a sharp change in defensive philosophy."[14]

In the months that followed early in 2012, when information from the Bountygate allegations began to surface, the NFL claimed that Sean Payton distrusted Gregg Williams to such an extent that Payton instructed Assistant Coach Joe Vitt to monitor Williams' activities.

The 8th line-itemed note from the NFL's official announcement on sanctions assessed to the Saints' coaches after Bountygate read: "Coach Vitt said one of his primary roles was to monitor the activity of Coach Williams. This was based on the direction of Coach Payton, who apparently had less than full confidence in Coach Williams."[15]

Clearly, a coaching change was in order for 2012.

***

With Gregg Williams having departed for St. Louis as the Rams' new defensive coordinator, the Saints once again looked to rebuild their defense. For 2012, the team focused their hiring efforts on Steve Spagnuolo, a highly-respected defensive coach.

Spagnuolo plied his trade under famed Philadelphia Eagles' defensive coordinator Jim Johnson, coaching the Eagles' secondary and linebackers for eight seasons.[16] From there, Spagnuolo served as the defensive coordinator for the New York Giants in 2007 and 2008, winning a Super Bowl in the process.

With his career trajectory upwardly mobile, Spagnuolo moved on to St. Louis where he was the Rams' head coach from 2009 - 2011. Spagnuolo failed in St. Louis, posting a miserable 10-38 record as head coach in three seasons. After the 2011 season, the Rams fired Spagnuolo.

Seeking to re-boot his career as a defensive specialist with a championship-caliber team, Spagnuolo signed with the Saints in late January 2012 as the team's newest defensive coordinator. At the time, this was an undeniable victory for the Saints. To land a defensive coordinator of Spagnuolo's pedigree, to pair him with the league's preeminent offensive mind was *the* recipe for the Saints to return to the Super Bowl.

Among the Saints' fanbase, Spagnuolo's arrival was viewed almost reverentially.

Upon calling to accept the Saints' offer to lead their 2012 defense, Steve Spagnuolo first said to Sean Payton "let's go win a Super Bowl"[17] before even saying "hello."

By all accounts, this was a perfect marriage of timing, need, and opportunity.

Future evidence, however, would prove otherwise.

2: march 2, 2012, the arrival of bountygate

Had Steve Spagnuolo known what would unfold a month after his hiring, he almost surely would have had misgivings about joining the Saints.

On a mundane Friday afternoon during the NFL's slumbering offseason, out of nowhere, the NFL dropped the atom bomb forever known as Bountygate.

It was a shocking announcement, delivered with maximum effect by the league and its media army.

In short, the NFL accused the Saints of maintaining a three-year program that rewarded Saints' defensive players for targeting and injuring opponents. A "bounty program," they said.

The entirety of the NFL's original statement on Bountygate read:

> A lengthy investigation by the NFL's security department has disclosed that between 22 and 27 defensive players on the New Orleans Saints, as well as at least one assistant coach, maintained a "bounty" program funded primarily by players in violation of NFL rules during the 2009, 2010 and 2011 seasons, the NFL announced today.
>
> The league's investigation determined that this improper "Pay for Performance" program included "bounty" payments to players for inflicting injuries on opposing players that would result in them being removed from a game.
>
> The findings - corroborated by multiple independent sources - have been presented to Commissioner Roger Goodell, who will determine the appropriate discipline for the violation.
>
> "The payments here are particularly troubling because they involved not just payments for 'performance,' but also for injuring opposing players," Commissioner Goodell said. "The bounty rule promotes two key elements of NFL football: player safety and competitive integrity.
>
> "It is our responsibility to protect player safety and the integrity of our game, and this type of conduct will not be tolerated. We have made significant progress in changing the culture with respect to

player safety and we are not going to relent. We have more work to do and we will do it."

The players regularly contributed cash into a pool and received improper cash payments of two kinds from the pool based on their play in the previous week's game. Payments were made for plays such as interceptions and fumble recoveries, but the program also included "bounty" payments for "cart-offs" (meaning that the opposing player was carried off the field) and "knockouts" (meaning that the opposing player was not able to return to the game).

The investigation showed that the total amount of funds in the pool may have reached $50,000 or more at its height during the 2009 playoffs. The program paid players $1,500 for a "knockout" and $1,000 for a "cart-off" with payouts doubling or tripling during the playoffs.

The investigation included the review of approximately 18,000 documents totaling more than 50,000 pages, interviews of a wide range of individuals and the use of outside forensic experts to verify the authenticity of key documents.

The NFL has a longstanding rule prohibiting "Non-Contract Bonuses." Non-contract bonuses violate both the NFL Constitution and By-Laws and the Collective Bargaining Agreement. Clubs are advised every year of this rule in a memo from the commissioner. Citing Sections 9.1(8), and 9.3(F) and (G) of the Constitution and By-Laws, the memo for the 2011 season stated:

"No bonus or award may directly or indirectly be offered, promised, announced, or paid to a player for his or his team's performance against a particular team or opposing player or a particular group thereof. No bonuses or awards may be offered or paid for on field misconduct (for example, personal fouls to or injuries inflicted on opposing players)."

"Our investigation began in early 2010 when allegations were first made that Saints players had targeted opposing players, including Kurt Warner of the Cardinals and Brett Favre of the Vikings," Commissioner Goodell said. "Our security department interviewed numerous players and other individuals. At the time, those interviewed denied that any such program existed and the player that made the allegation retracted his earlier assertions. As a result, the allegations could not be proven. We recently received significant and credible new information and the investigation was re-opened during the latter part of the 2011 season."

The additional investigation established the following facts:

1. During the 2009, 2010 and 2011 seasons, the players and other participants involved used their own money to fund a "Pay for Performance" program. Players earned cash awards for plays such as interceptions or fumble recoveries. They also earned "bounty" payments for "cart-offs" and "knockouts." All such payments violate league rules for non-contract bonuses.

2. Players were willing and enthusiastic participants in the program, contributing regularly and at times pledging large amounts. Between 22 and 27 defensive players contributed funds to the pool over the course of three NFL seasons. In some cases, the amounts pledged were both significant and directed against a specific opposing player.

3. The bounty program was administered by defensive coordinator Gregg Williams with the knowledge of other defensive coaches. Funds were contributed on occasion by Williams.

4. Saints owner Tom Benson gave immediate and full cooperation to the investigators. The evidence conclusively established that Mr. Benson was not aware of the bounty program. When informed earlier this year of the new information, Mr. Benson advised league staff that he had directed his general manager, Mickey Loomis, to ensure that any bounty program be discontinued immediately. The evidence showed that Mr. Loomis did not carry out Mr. Benson's directions. Similarly, when the initial allegations were discussed with Mr. Loomis in 2010, he denied any knowledge of a bounty program and pledged that he would ensure that no such program was in place. There is no evidence that Mr. Loomis took any effective action to stop these practices.

5. Although head coach Sean Payton was not a direct participant in the funding or administration of the program, he was aware of the allegations, did not make any detailed inquiry or otherwise seek to learn the facts, and failed to stop the bounty program. He never instructed his assistant coaches or players that a bounty program was improper and could not continue.

6. There is no question that a bounty program violates long-standing league rules. Payments of this type - even for legitimate plays such as interceptions or fumble recoveries - are forbidden because they are inconsistent with the Collective Bargaining Agreement and well-accepted rules relating to NFL player contracts.

Commissioner Goodell has advised the Saints that he will hold further proceedings to determine the discipline to be assessed against individuals and the club. This will include conferring with the NFL Players Association and individual player leaders regarding appropriate discipline and remedial steps.

The discipline could include fines and suspensions and, in light of the competitive nature of the violation, forfeiture of draft choices. Any discipline may be appealed as provided for in the Constitution and By-Laws and Collective Bargaining Agreement. Any appeal would be heard and decided by the commissioner.

This was the NFL's first memo (of many) purporting to be evidence of malicious activity by the Saints. Positioned through the media as a multi-year, institutionalized pay-to-injure program, this allegation was both a misrepresentation of reality and a distortion of facts from the very beginning.

As we learned as the process unfolded in the subsequent months, NFL press releases and league-drafted memos were pawned off as unassailable "evidence," bolstered by an enabling media who largely refused to do anything but blindly legitimize the NFL's non-vetted claims.[18]

The coaches and players intent on defending themselves against these allegations were repeatedly denied access to the empirical source evidence that the NFL had supposedly collected among its 50,000 pages of documentation. Only many months later, when much of the damage had already been done, did the NFL slowly leak out its weak stream of flaccid evidence used to indict the accused.

In the place of true evidence, memos and press releases served to implicate the accused and inform the general public, no matter how specious or distorting.

In this original statement, the NFL accused between 22 and 27 players of wrongdoing, yet ultimately punished only four. Further, in an investigation labeled as comprehensive and wide-ranging and conducted by "forensic experts," the NFL failed the most basic test of simply identifying an exact number of alleged participants.

That a nebulous range of players was implicated, and then only four punished, illuminated the tenuous state of the NFL's investigation and evidence.

This was but a small sample of systemic shortcomings, and only the beginning of questioning the credibility and legitimacy of the NFL's investigation and motives. Over the course of this book, I'll examine the flawed evidence in full as we encounter it during Bountygate's chronology. But these basic defects in the NFL's initial statement provided insight into an investigation fraught with ulterior motive, glaring flaws, outright lies, opacity, and a reliance on disgruntled witnesses of unreliable credibility.

The fix was in.

By vociferously and publicly accusing the Saints before due process ran its course, in the absence of even the most basic standards of transparency, by selectively crafting a message of "changing the culture,"[19] the NFL had set in motion a campaign designed to trumpet its dedication -- no matter how disingenuous -- to "player safety"[20] and "competitive integrity."[21]

As I'll examine later, there was clear and ample motive for the NFL's Bountygate crusade, regardless of the veracity of their allegations.

At its root, Bountygate was the perfect storm of the NFL using a franchise perceived as intransigent to further its own ends and protect its brand.

The Saints were both the facilitators and collateral damage of this misguided, unjust strategy.

***

Inviting more skepticism to the initial allegations of Bountygate was this important factor:

Why did the NFL choose to make public this "scandal" when they could have handled it privately? This was an NFL investigation, not one of an independent body, and it was the NFL's decision to publicize this information in a very big way.

At first glance, the NFL being publicly connected to activity injurious to the health of its players ran counter to the league's interests at a time when they faced litigation for failing to protect players from the long-term consequences of concussions.

Why would the NFL voluntarily release this information when it seemed harmful to them?

In a *Miami Herald* article by Dan Le Batard titled *"Roger Goodell cares more for cash than safety,"* [22] Le Batard said this soon after Bountygate's arrival:

> ... the Saints bounty story has been so different, prepared and packaged for our consumption by the NFL. That's unusual ... Goodell clearly wants this in the news. He wants people to be shocked and outraged and clucking. And, yes, safety is his primary concern ... if by that you mean keeping his league safe from lawsuits. This is all a shield for his shield, you might say.

> First, in this media age when no one can keep a secret, nobody broke the Saints bounties story. The NFL volunteered it. Revealed it in an announcement after a private investigation. How often does that happen, exactly?

> ... Goodell doesn't want this buried. Quite the opposite. He wants his handling of this out in front of everybody for as long as he can keep it there. That's why the NFL's initial release went out of its way to use the word "bounty." That'll get the media's attention every time. Call it a "big-hit pool" instead of a "bounty," and you've got a nation of football fans shrugging instead of a national debate about right and wrong.

What Le Batard intimated was this: the NFL manufactured a crisis -- or at least distorted a smaller issue out of proportion -- and then presented it to the general public in an effort to proclaim the league's dedication to protecting the safety of its players.

Further, the timing of the original announcement reinforced Le Batard's point. Coming at a naturally slow period for NFL news, in between the Super Bowl and the draft, the NFL released the Bountygate accusations to a captive audience insatiably ravenous for NFL news year-round.

Was the timing a coincidence? Or was it a premeditated tactic?

Either way, the reactions it generated set the football world abuzz.

3: the football world reacts

Reactions to the Bountygate allegations were swift, hysterical, hyperbolic, and largely one-sided.

In what became a defining characteristic of this scandal, a disproportionate focus of the media narrative centered on moralizing, casting judgment, settling scores, and failing to hold the NFL accountable to verifiable truths.

By December of 2012, when Paul Tagliabue voided the players' suspensions, *Sports Illustrated's* Jim Trotter echoed this sentiment, saying:[23] "Tagliabue's ruling is also a rebuke of the media. Many of us were quick to accept the league's allegations as fact, just because."

As such, the NFL media (in large, though not in full) presided over the proceedings with a presumption of Saints' guilt; disregarded the importance of facts; and routinely wielded unsubstantiations as dogma. They mostly rushed to demonize the Saints, chastise Sean Payton, vilify Jonathan Vilma, and blindly validate the NFL's accusations.

On the night the bounty allegations broke, before the media and the public had anything more than a one-sided NFL press release to inform them of the "facts," in a silly, off-target display of misinformed condemnation, *The Times Picayune's* Jeff Duncan wrote:[24]

> Make no mistake, this is a black eye for the organization. Their lone Super Bowl title is forever tarnished, their squeaky-clean image irreparable (sic) harmed …
>
> The Saints will now rank alongside the Spygate Patriots and cocky Cowboys among the most despised teams in the NFL. This story will follow the Saints for years. It's not going to go away after the league hands down its punishment.
>
> It also will tarnish the legacy of owner Tom Benson, who appeared to do everything right in this case yet was failed by the men he entrusted to lead his organization. Loomis and Payton were derelict in their duties.
>
> This wasn't a one-time indiscretion. This was organized, institutionalized system of improper behavior and actions that

took place over an extended period and condoned by team leaders ...

In this case, not even the Saints can expect salvation.

Their punishment will be harsh. It will be extensive. And it will be just.

Just hours after the initial allegations, in sweeping judgment, Duncan decided that the Saints were inarguably guilty.

Basing his judgment on an NFL memo of unknown veracity, Duncan faultily reasoned that the Saints, their Super Bowl title, and their owner were forever "tarnished."

Missing the point, Duncan referenced justice in his last sentence. Yet it was Duncan's contention that the due process and transparency owed to the team and players -- pillars of ensuring *actual* justice -- need not be a part of determining guilt in this case.

To him, the verdict was already in: the NFL's claims were irrefutable dogma. Simply because Roger Goodell and the NFL levied damning accusations, and before the extent of the sanctions was even known, the outcome would nevertheless be "just" in Duncan's opinion.

Calling Duncan's reaction both a rush to judgment and an astonishing failure would be a fair critique.

And Duncan wasn't alone.

A mere two days after the original allegations, *ESPN's* Ashley Fox called for the firings of both Sean Payton and Mickey Loomis.

Like Duncan, Fox based the entirety of her argument on an NFL press release and recklessly lobbied for career-threatening outcomes for Payton and Loomis, all while being only marginally informed.

The opening of Fox's article[25] read: "Sean Payton deserves to get fired. Mickey Loomis does, too."

In her article Fox railed against the "stupidity and arrogance" of Payton and Loomis, as though shortcomings in character -- true or not -- justified two men losing their jobs after being railroaded by a corrupt process.

CBS's Mike Freeman, on the afternoon the bounty allegations broke,[26] took to calling Saints' players "hypocrites" and "phonies." After calling for the firings of Payton and Loomis, Freeman revealed his inherent bias towards Sean Payton when he said "[t]here are many reasons not to like Payton; this is just another."

Instead of practicing any modicum of professional objectivity towards the events in question, Freeman feebly resorted to personal attacks and name-calling.

In what might be the most regrettable sentence written by a member of the media in the aftermath of Bountygate, Freeman said: "This is, to me, perhaps the finest hour for Goodell."

That Roger Goodell would ultimately have an appeals' board reverse the players' punishments; that a federal judge would admonish Goodell for his actions; that former NFL Commissioner Paul Tagliabue would permanently void the players' punishments all reiterated that this was anything but the "finest hour" for Goodell. On the contrary, it revealed utter failure.

In step with his colleagues on the afternoon of March 2nd, Clark Judge of *CBS* said the NFL should[27] "make [the Saints] suffer" because "now we have evidence from the NFL office that what the Saints did was illegal."

For Judge, an NFL press release equated to "evidence" that should be righteously used to inflict pain on the Saints' organization. Not only was it revealing that Judge wrongly believed this original memo was "evidence," but his retributive reflex of advocating "[suffering]" read more like demagoguery and much less like reporting.

Like his colleagues, Judge eschewed the importance of transparency and impartiality before casting judgment; he simply took the NFL's word as gospel and moralized accordingly.

Perhaps the most egregious example of this reactionary, off-target journalism came from *SI's* Peter King. In a March 12th edition of *Sports Illustrated*, the magazine headlined a King story dubbed "*Bounty Culture.*"[28] A subheading of King's article read "The Saints pay-to-injure program rattles the NFL."

Jonathan Vilma appeared on the cover of the magazine, wrongly vilified, unfairly posterized, and presented with a presumption of guilt by both King and *SI*.

Particularly damning was *SI's* use of the phrase "pay-to-injure," a false allegation that distorted the reality of the events. Further, in his obsequious quest to validate Goodell's claims, King fell down the rabbit hole of hyperbole and compared the Saints' budding scandal to Watergate, an investigation's truth that, ironically, was uncovered by ferocious watchdog journalism.

In this instance, King was practicing anything but. Instead of looking for the truth and asking meaningful questions, King opted to weakly parrot the NFL's claims in a defining moment of slavish myopia.

Equally important, King laid out a series of specific allegations in his article -- made public for the first time -- that were eventually proven untrue, unreliable, or dismissed entirely by the NFL. But before that could happen, King shared these accusations:

1.) The alleged $10,000 bounty on Brett Favre

2.) Anthony Hargrove demanding payment for the alleged Favre bounty

3.) An intimation of a bounty on Kurt Warner

4.) An email from Mike Ornstein supposedly pledging a bounty on Aaron Rodgers in a 2011 game

5.) The inclusion of Scott Fujita as a guilty participant

While I'll deconstruct in detail the flaws and unreliability of these allegations later in the book, it's safe to say that each of the claims that King presented as evidence of guilt turned out to be unreliable or blatantly false.

***

In the days immediately following the original Bountygate allegations, the large majority of the NFL media failed badly.

Large, influential organizations like *ESPN, SI, CBS Sports,* and *The Times Picayune* shaped public perception based on incomplete and faulty information. They reached conclusions before being fully-informed. They reacted personally and vindictively. They assumed guilt by the Saints, and fostered an atmosphere of infallibility for the NFL's claims.

It was shameful and cowardice.

In the meantime, the reputations and careers of the accused hung in the balance.

***

While the media reacted swiftly to the Bountygate allegations, the accused were a bit slower to react.

In its original statement, the NFL specifically identified Gregg Williams, Sean Payton, Mickey Loomis, and "other defensive coaches" as guilty parties. The players who would eventually be punished -- Jonathan Vilma, Anthony Hargrove, Will Smith, and Scott Fujita -- had not yet been officially identified by league.

On March 2nd, the day of the allegations, Gregg Williams released his first of two statements. In full, it read:[29]

> I want to express my sincere regret and apology to the NFL, Mr. Benson, and the New Orleans Saints fans for my participation in the "pay for performance" program while I was with the Saints.
>
> It was a terrible mistake, and we knew it was wrong while we were doing it. Instead of getting caught up in it, I should have stopped it. I take full responsibility for my role. I am truly sorry. I have learned a hard lesson and I guarantee that I will never participate in or allow this kind of activity to happen again.

Aside from the mild, professionally-drafted tone of the statement, the noteworthy facet of Williams' apology resided in his usage of the term "pay-for-performance," sharply contrasting to the NFL's allegation of a "bounty" program and *SI's* corroborating accusation of a "pay-to-injure" system.

The differentiation in this terminology became an important factor in how the NFL and its media shaped the Saints' purported misdeeds in the public arena. Where a "pay-for-performance" system simply rewarded legal plays, a "bounty/pay-to-injure" program inferred the targeting of specific opponents for the express purposes of injury.

From the outset, Saints' coaches and players repeatedly denied targeting and injuring opponents while, at the same time, conceded to operating a pay-for-performance system. This admission by the Saints has been misconstrued in fan and media circles as culpability for institutionalized injury activity, which was not the case.

This distinction lies at the heart of Bountygate, and the NFL's distortion of this terminology -- and what it factually entailed -- bolstered the league's public campaign to cast the Saints in a malicious light.

One of the first individuals to publicly refute the NFL's claims against the Saints was Duke Naipohn, a consultant and fatigue risk management specialist who spent the majority of the 2011 season with the Saints.

Naipohn worked closely with Gregg Williams during 2011 and traveled with the team for a large majority of the year, a season in which the NFL claimed the Saints were operating a bounty program. Of the allegations, Naipohn said:[30]

> None of that was going on. There was no calling out of names, there was never, "We're going to take this guy out," and here's $5,000, nothing like that ...
>
> Players were making side bets. You know, "'I'll get a pick before you," or "I'll get a pick and you won't," or "I'll have more red zone tackles than you," big plays ...
>
> A bounty program that pays a bonus for injuring another player is a ruthless conspiracy and should be eliminated. And anyone who contributed to the look-the-other-way approach to policing this kind of behavior should also be punished. However, that's not what happened in the Saints' team meeting rooms or locker rooms or any of the places I was at.
>
> There was no one standing up, throwing dollars down and challenging anyone to hurt someone. That's just simply speculation and sensationalistic. I was there to witness every minutes (sic) of it, and that's not what happened.

Among the mounting claims and speculation in the press, Naipohn's response gained little traction even after he reiterated this statement to an NFL investigator and ex-FBI agent. Apparently, it was testimony the NFL wasn't interested in hearing.

On March 13th former Saint Tracy Porter also weighed in,[31] explained the differences between the Saints' pay-for-performance system and the accusations of bounties, and supported Naipohn's assertions along the way.

Porter said:

> ... it wasn't a thing of going out and saying, "We're going to hurt this guy, we're going to hurt that guy." We came out saying, you know, "You make an impactful play then you get compensated for it."
>
> That's something that we had in-house. But there was never any ... I can sit here and say there was never any bounty where we said, "Oh we're going to go out there and hurt this guy."

While conventional wisdom mounted in regards to the Saints' guilt -- an inevitable result of the NFL's powerful media campaign -- a counter-narrative developed as Saints' insiders began to tell their side of the story.

4: saints' coaches, organization punished

On March 21st, 19 days after the NFL released its Bountygate accusations, Roger Goodell dispensed historic punishments to the Saints' organization and the coaches allegedly involved.

In short, the punishments were:

* Saints: $500,000 fine, forfeiture of 2012 & 2013 second-round draft picks

* Sean Payton: suspended without pay for the 2012 season, effective April 1st

* Mickey Loomis: suspended without pay for the first eight games of the 2012 regular season

* Gregg Williams: suspended indefinitely from the NFL, effective immediately; reinstatement after the 2012 season dependent on his cooperation with the NFL's investigation going forward, at Roger Goodell's discretion

* Joe Vitt: suspended without pay for the first six games of the 2012 regular season

Prior to these sanctions, no NFL coach had been suspended for even one game. In a fell swoop, Goodell rained down an unprecedented 38 games of coaching suspensions.

In full, the NFL released fifteen findings when they announced these penalties:[32]

> 1. The Saints defensive team operated a pay-for-performance/bounty program, primarily funded by players, during the 2009, 2010, and 2011 seasons. Under that program, players regularly made cash "donations" to a pool, and were "fined" for mental errors, loafing, penalties, and the like. At least one assistant coach (defensive coordinator Gregg Williams) also occasionally contributed to the pool. There is no evidence that any club money was contributed to the program.
>
> 2. Payments were made for plays such as interceptions or fumble recoveries. All such payments are against league rules. Payments also were made for plays on which opposing players

were injured. In addition, specific players were sometimes targeted. The investigation showed bounties being placed on four quarterbacks of opposing teams - Brett Favre, Cam Newton, Aaron Rodgers, and Kurt Warner. Multiple sources have confirmed that several players pledged funds toward bounties on specific opposing players, with defensive captain Jonathan Vilma offering $10,000 to any player who knocked Brett Favre out of the NFC Championship Game in 2010.

3. Coach Williams acknowledged that he designed and implemented the program with the assistance of certain defensive players. He said that he did so after being told by Saints Head Coach Sean Payton that his assignment was to make the defense "nasty." Coach Williams described his role as overseeing record keeping, defining payout amounts, deciding on who received payouts, and distributing envelopes with cash to players who "earned" rewards.

4. In each of the 2009-2011 seasons, the Saints were one of the top five teams in the league in roughing the passer penalties. In 2009 and 2011, the Saints were also in the top five teams in unnecessary roughness penalties; in 2010, the Saints ranked sixth in the category. In the January 16, 2010 divisional playoff game against the Arizona Cardinals, Saints defensive players were assessed $15,000 in fines for fouls committed against opposing players. The following week, in the NFC Championship Game against the Minnesota Vikings, Saints defensive players were assessed $30,000 in fines for four separate illegal hits, several of which were directed against quarterback Brett Favre.

5. Coach Williams now acknowledges that when he was first questioned about this matter in early 2010 he intentionally misled NFL investigators and made no effort to stop the program after he became aware of the league's investigation.

6. Coach Williams further confirmed that the program continued during the 2010 and 2011 seasons, and that he occasionally contributed funds to the pool in each of those seasons.

7. Assistant Head Coach/Defense Joe Vitt acknowledged that he was aware of the program in 2009-2011. He admitted that, when interviewed in 2010, he "fabricated the truth" to NFL investigators and denied that any pay-for-performance or bounty program existed at the Saints.

8. Coach Vitt said one of his primary roles was to monitor the activity of Coach Williams. This was based on the direction of Coach Payton, who apparently had less than full confidence in Coach Williams. Despite Coach Vitt's knowledge of the bounty program, his understanding of the terms "knock-out" and "cart-off," his witnessing Coach Williams handing out envelopes that he believed to contain cash, and his acknowledgement that the defensive meeting preceding the 2010 NFC Championship Game may have "got out of hand" with respect to Brett Favre, Coach Vitt claimed he never advised either Coach Payton or General Manager Mickey Loomis of the "pay-for-performance/bounty" program.

9. A summary prepared following a Saints preseason game included the statement, "1 Cart-off - Crank up the John Deer (sic) Tractor" in reference to a hit on an opposing player. Similar statements are reflected in prepared documents or slides in connection with other games in multiple seasons. A review of the game films confirms that opposing players were injured on the plays identified in the documents.

10. When interviewed in 2012, Sean Payton claimed to be entirely unaware of the program, a claim contradicted by others. Further, prior to the Saints' opening game in 2011, Coach Payton received an email from a close associate that stated in part, "PS Greg Williams put me down for $5000 on Rogers (sic)." When shown the email during the course of the investigation, Coach Payton stated that it referred to a "bounty" on Green Bay quarterback Aaron Rodgers.

11. In early 2010, Mr. Loomis advised Coach Payton that the league office was investigating allegations concerning a bounty program. Coach Payton said that he met with his top two defensive assistants, Coach Williams and Coach Vitt, in advance of the interview with league investigators and told them, "Let's make sure our ducks are in a row." Remarkably, Coach Payton claimed that he never inquired of Coach Williams and Coach Vitt as to what happened in the interviews, never asked them if a "pay-for-performance" or bounty program was in fact in place, and never gave any instructions to discontinue such a program.

12. In January 2012, prior to the Saints' first playoff game of the 2011 season, Coach Payton was advised by Mr. Loomis that the league office had reopened the investigation. Coach Payton

made a cursory inquiry but took no action to ensure that any bounty program was discontinued.

13. General Manager Mickey Loomis was not present at meetings of the Saints defense at which bounties were discussed and was not aware of bounties being placed on specific players. Mr. Loomis became aware of the allegations regarding a bounty program no later than February 2010 when he was notified of the investigation into the allegations during a meeting with NFL Executive Vice President-Football Operations Ray Anderson. He was directed to ensure that any such program ceased immediately. By his own admission, Mr. Loomis did not do enough to determine if a pay-for-performance/bounty program existed or to end any such program that did exist.

14. Saints owner Tom Benson notified Mr. Loomis in January 2012 prior to the team's participation in the playoffs that the league's investigation had been reopened. Mr. Benson reiterated his position that a bounty program was unacceptable and instructed Mr. Loomis to ensure that if a bounty program existed at the Saints it would stop immediately. By his own admission, Mr. Loomis responded to this direction by making only cursory inquiries of Coaches Payton and Williams. He never issued instructions to end the bounty program to either the coaching staff or the players.

15. There is no evidence that Saints ownership had any knowledge of the pay-for-performance or bounty program. There is no evidence that any club funds were used for the program. Ownership made clear that it disapproved of the program, gave prompt and clear direction that it stop, and gave full and immediate cooperation to league investigators.

Of particular note in these findings are the following four claims:

A.) In line item two, the NFL claimed the Saints placed bounties on four opposing quarterbacks: Brett Favre, Kurt Warner, Aaron Rodgers, and Cam Newton.

By December when Paul Tagliabue conducted Bountygate's final appeals' hearing, there was no mention of or evidence corroborating a bounty placed on Warner, Rodgers, or Newton. The associated claims had vanished from the NFL's allegations at that point.

In the NFL's final Bountygate contentions -- many months later -- three of these bounty accusations were not even worthy of their initial alleged nature, and thus not included as evidence of wrongdoing.

The allegation of the Favre bounty Tagliabue largely dismissed, saying:[33]

> There was no evidence that Vilma or anyone else paid any money to any player for any bounty-related hit on an opposing player in the Vikings game ...
>
> ... there is no evidence that a player's speech prior to a game was actually a factor causing misconduct on the playing field and that such misconduct was severe enough in itself to warrant a player suspension or a very substantial fine.

Much more on this event later.

B.) The fourth line item, citing penalty data, attempted to identify the Saints as one of the NFL's most malicious teams from 2009 - 2011.

However, an independent study of injury data in the NFL during the 2009 - 2011 seasons refuted the NFL's claim. Economists Kevin Hassett and Stan Veuger produced a comprehensive, independent report that determined the inflicted injury rates of all 32 NFL teams from 2009 - 2011.

Both Ivy-league educated, both employed by the American Enterprise Institute, Hassett and Veuger found that the Saints injured fewer players than all but one team in the league (San Diego Chargers) during the three seasons the NFL accused them of operating a targeted injury program.

Appearing in the *L.A. Times*, Hassett's and Veuger's conclusions read:[34]

> Did the New Orleans Saints injure more players?
>
> The data-driven answer is a resounding "no." The Saints appear to have injured far fewer players over the 2009, 2010 and 2011 seasons. The numbers are striking. From 2009 to 2011, the Saints injured, on average, 3.2 opposing players each game. The rest of the teams in the league caused, on average, 3.8 injuries per game. This difference is highly statistically significant, or in other words, it would hold up in a court of law or a fancy academic journal.

In each year of the bounty program, the Saints injured fewer players than the average for the league. In 2009, the Saints injured 2.8 players a game, and other teams injured on average 3.8. In 2010, it was 3.5 and 3.6, and in 2011 it was 3.3 and 3.8.

The Saints' behavior on the field was certainly aberrant, but positively so. Only one other team, the San Diego Chargers, injured fewer opponents per game over this entire time frame (3.1 injuries).

The question, then, was simple.

If the Saints maintained an institutionalized injury program for three seasons, then why did they injure fewer players than all but one team did during this time frame?

Did the players fail to follow their coaches' orders? Were they incompetent? Or was there no pay-to-injure program in place?

C.) The NFL's ninth finding, "prepared documents" that contained payments for injuries, was the first mention of what would soon be better known as the "bounty ledger."

As we'll see, the claims associated with this ledger would be roundly debunked.

As a result, the NFL ultimately failed to submit this ledger as an official exhibit in their evidence against the players. Like the alleged bounties on Warner, Rodgers, and Newton, the NFL discarded this ledger as evidence in the months after it was presented to the public.

D.) In line item ten, the NFL implicated Mike Ornstein as a participant in Bountygate, citing an email he supposedly sent to Sean Payton pledging a bounty on Aaron Rodgers.

And though the NFL claimed in its memo Payton acknowledged a bounty on Rodgers, plenty of the NFL's claims in this report were off-base. Further, Peter King reported[35] this: "Confronted with the e-mail from Ornstein, Payton expressed surprise and said he hadn't read the e-mail."

Much more on the details of this email later.

***

On the same day the NFL announced these punishments, Gregg Williams had a second statement[36] (apology) at the ready. Released this time by the St. Louis Rams, Williams' statement, in full, read:

> I'd like to again apologize wholeheartedly to the NFL, Coach Fisher, the entire Rams organization and all football fans for my action. Furthermore, I apologize to the players of the NFL for my involvement as it is not a true reflection of my values as a father or coach, nor is it reflective of the great respect I have for this game and its core principle of sportsmanship. I accept full responsibility for my actions. I highly value the 23 years that I've spent in the NFL.
>
> I will continue to cooperate fully with the league and its investigation and I will focus my energies on serving as an advocate for both player safety and sportsmanship. I will do everything possible to re-earn the respect of my colleagues, the NFL and its players in hopes of returning to coaching in the future.

Though most of this statement appeared to be public relations' boilerplate, the noteworthy aspect was Williams' intent to "cooperate fully with the league and its investigation." This sentiment wasn't included in Williams' first statement, and its inclusion suggested that this newer statement was strongly influenced by the NFL.

After all, the NFL had made clear hours earlier that Williams' reinstatement was dependent on his cooperation. Here, Williams ensured he was on board with the NFL's directives.

Three days later, on March 24th, Sean Payton released a statement of his own.[37] Much less specific, Payton said:

> I share and fully support the league's concerns and goals on player safety. It is, and should be, paramount. Respecting our great game and the NFL shield is extremely important to me.
>
> Our organization will implement all necessary protections and protocols, and I will be more vigilant going forward. I am sorry for what has happened and as head coach take full responsibility. Finally, I want to thank Mr. Benson, our players and all Saints fans for their overwhelming support.

Notably, Payton took "full responsibility." But for what, he didn't specify.

The fact, though, that the word "bounty" nor "injury" ever appeared in the combined three statements released by Gregg Williams and Sean Payton was telling. There was never an admission that targeted injury was ever a facet of the Saints' incentive program.

Moreover, Williams' first statement specifically referenced a "pay-for-performance," not a "bounty," system.

Equally revealing, the two post-punishment statements both specifically mentioned "player safety," presumably the chief message the NFL intended to highlight via its bounty accusations.

***

What's important to remember about these findings, and the league's resulting discipline, is that a league-drafted memo served as the "evidence" that resulted in the unprecedented sanctions levied upon the coaches and the Saints' organization.

The coaches were never presented with any source evidence. The process entailed a "he said/she said" proposition, with the coaches unable to refute the veracity of the NFL's claims or face their accusers.

The NFL simply accused the coaches of engaging in activity of a nebulous nature, drafted an internal memo that supported their claims, refused to share any actual evidence behind those claims, then punished the coaches at their behest.

Without the protection of a union, the coaches were at the mercy of Roger Goodell and the league. Moreover, as both Payton and Williams were solely dependent on Roger Goodell for reinstatement, their NFL careers suddenly hung in the balance. Had they decided to fight back or publicly refute the claims with no legal basis to protect them, Payton and Williams risked ending their NFL careers.

As we'd see with the accused players, a vastly different process would unfold when bolstered by the players' legal protections. For Payton and Williams, it was the NFL's way or no way at all.

So they didn't buck.

Furthermore, Gregg Williams' position was even more troubling. The NFL specifically noted[38] that Williams' reinstatement was dependent upon "the extent to which [he] cooperate[d] with the NFL in any further proceedings."

With starkly coercive language, the NFL virtually ensured that Williams would participate in a manner that was palatable to them. It was almost certainly important for the NFL to eliminate the likelihood that the outspoken Williams would go public with his opinion on the accusations.

As such, basing Williams' reinstatement on cooperation would allow the NFL to shape Williams' role going forward in a manner most beneficial to their preferred outcome.

Less than a month into this quagmire, Bountygate's surface had barely been scratched.

5: the brees' negotiations

In the midst of the cacophony of March when the Bountygate accusations surfaced, Drew Brees was in the process of negotiating a new contract with the Saints.

In 2006 Brees signed a six-year, $60 million contract with the Saints. When he played that contract to its completion after the 2011 season, Brees was set to be a free agent in 2012.

By this point in his career, Brees had established himself as one of the league's preeminent quarterbacks: a Super Bowl MVP; the NFL's most prolific modern passer; and the face of the Saints' franchise. With Sean Payton, Brees was largely responsible for reversing the heretofore malodorous fortunes of the Saints.

On top of his many other accomplishments, Brees had just submitted the greatest passing season in NFL history.[39] In 2011, Brees set NFL records for passing yards in a season (5,476) and completion percentage in a season (71.2%). He also threw 46 touchdowns, the fourth best single-season mark in NFL history.

Now, with the Saints in crisis, Brees was unsigned and away from the team.

On March 3rd, just one day after the Bountygate allegations broke, the Saints placed the "exclusive rights" franchise tag[40] on Brees, preventing him from negotiating with other teams. Though this protected the Saints from losing Brees, it wasn't without peril.

Because teams can only tag (i.e., protect) one player per season, the Saints allowed two players of critical importance -- Marques Colston and Carl Nicks -- to enter the free agent market with no restrictions. They were both free to negotiate and sign with other teams.

Colston was well on his way to being the most productive wide receiver in Saints' history, and Carl Nicks was widely regarded as one of the NFL's best offensive guards. With Brees tagged, the Saints faced the prospect of losing both Colston and Nicks to other teams.

What was frustrating about Brees' contract situation was that it had reached this stage. Top-performing quarterbacks, like Brees, often have their contracts renegotiated before expiration in order to:

eliminate the possibility of a holdout; secure longer-term security at a better salary; and ensure the player's long-term future with the team. By the end of the 2009 season, when Brees had delivered a Super Bowl title to New Orleans and amassed (at the time) only the second 5,000-yard passing season in NFL history,[41] Brees had unquestionably outplayed his contract.

As early as February 4th, 2010, *ESPN's* Adam Schefter reported[42] that Brees and the Saints would renegotiate the quarterback's current contract prior to the 2010 regular season. Schefter said:

> New Orleans considered extending Brees' contract last offseason, but opted to wait another year. Now that it has, the price only has risen with Brees performing the way he has. Should the Saints win Super Bowl XLIV, Brees practically would be able to name his price.
>
> Discussions on a new deal have yet to begin, but they will this offseason. A contract is expected to be wrapped up by the time the Saints report to training camp if not during it, but nobody around the league expects Brees to play the 2010 season under the six-year, $60 million contract that he signed in March 2006.

For whatever reason, that didn't come to fruition.

When the NFL locked out its players during the 2011 offseason while negotiating a new collective bargaining agreement, Brees and the Saints delayed contract negotiations. By the time the 2011 regular season had started, Brees suspended negotiations in order to focus on the season. And by March of 2012, the Saints' franchise quarterback was no longer under contract with the team.

Now the Saints were faced with making Brees the highest-paid player in the NFL, in the same offseason where salary cap flexibility was limited and several other key players were due for new contracts (Colston, Nicks, Tracy Porter, and Robert Meachem among others).

***

In a rare moment of seasonal reprieve, the Saints re-signed Marques Colston to a long-term deal on March 13th. A day later, however, Carl Nicks departed for division rival Tampa Bay after signing a contract that made him the highest-paid guard in the NFL.

The loss to the Saints was significant, at least temporarily.

Complicating matters was the Bountygate fiasco. The Saints were swept up in a swirl of controversy; Sean Payton would soon be banished for the season; and with Brees away from the team due to contract negotiations, the void of leadership in the Saints' organization became more glaring on a daily basis.

In an offseason of unprecedented distractions, Brees' absence was yet another contributing factor.

6: the parcells' flirtation

With Sean Payton's year-long suspension looming, the Saints faced the unfortunate task of selecting an interim coach for 2012.

Payton was scheduled for exile from the NFL starting on April 1st. Considering that Roger Goodell handed down Payton's penalty on March 21st, there wasn't much time to build contingencies *(note: Payton's year-long suspension would ultimately start on April 16th)*.

Worse, the 2012 NFL Draft was set for April 26th. Without Payton involved, and without first and second round picks, the Saints' draft prospects appeared dim at a time when the Saints were up against the salary cap, and the need for drafting affordable, young talent was as important as ever.

In the span of not much more than a week, Payton had a lot to do and not nearly enough time to do it.

When it came to identifying a replacement coach for Payton, the options were aplenty. First, the Saints had just hired Steve Spagnuolo who was fresh off of a three-year stint as the St. Louis Rams' head coach. Though Spagnuolo's tenure in St. Louis wasn't exactly a rousing success, he was nevertheless intimately familiar with the routine of running an NFL team. In a pinch, he would do.

Besides Spagnuolo the Saints possessed two talented offensive coaches in Pete Carmichael, Jr. and Aaron Kromer. Both Carmichael and Kromer seemed to be on the cusp of landing their own head coaching jobs in the near future. Early in the 2012 offseason, Pete Carmichael, Jr. interviewed for the Oakland Raiders' head coaching job,[43] while Kromer interviewed for the St. Louis Rams' vacancy.[44]

In particular, Carmichael seemed like a suitable replacement for Payton. In week six of the 2011 season, Sean Payton suffered a serious knee injury when Jimmy Graham collided with Payton on the sideline. For the next month, Payton was absent from the Saints' sideline due to the limitations of his movement.

In a foreboding twist, the Saints effectively had a trial run without Payton. Absent the team for stretches while rehabbing his knee in 2011, Payton delegated many of his routine tasks to his assistants. As a result, Carmichael handled a heavy portion of the offensive in-week gameplanning, while Joe Vitt conducted practice sessions.

Unbeknownst to Saints' fans, or anyone else for that matter, 2011 provided a glimpse of what was to come.

In the four games in 2011 when Payton wasn't on the sideline, Carmichael assumed playcalling duties -- previously the sole domain of Payton, widely considered the NFL's best playcaller. Joe Vitt handled the in-game management duties that Payton normally conducted.

With Carmichael calling plays for the second half of the 2011 season, the Saints' offense exploded. In the ten regular season games that Carmichael called plays, the Saints averaged 37 points and 476 yards per game, both league-high clips. That Payton had the confidence to surrender playcalling duties to Carmichael for the remainder of the 2011 season was an endorsement of the highest order.

So when Roger Goodell banished Sean Payton for the 2012 season, Carmichael seemed like a natural fit as Payton's replacement.

***

A lesser-known candidate for the role of interim coach was Aaron Kromer. The Saints' offensive line coach and running game coordinator since 2008, Kromer was a Jon Gruden protégé having coached under Gruden in both Oakland and Tampa Bay.

During his tenure in New Orleans, Kromer had assembled and coached one of the NFL's best offensive lines and had led the Saints' running game to top-six rankings in both 2009 and 2011. The rationale behind the potential selection of Kromer resided in allowing both Carmichael and Spagnuolo to retain their sole foci on running the offense and defense. As the thinking went, Kromer would slide into the head coaching spot while the offense and defense maintained a level of consistency and focus that wouldn't be far removed the norm.

Rounding out the Saints' internal candidates to replace Sean Payton was Joe Vitt. A football lifer, Vitt served as the Saints linebackers' coach since 2006 and was the de facto consigliere to Payton for many years. Vitt had experience in an interim head coaching role,[45] leading the St. Louis Rams for the last eleven games of the 2005 season after a heart infection sidelined head coach Mike Martz.

The obvious problem facing Vitt's potential appointment as interim coach was his own suspension, which would keep Vitt out for the first six games of 2012.

The question lingered: who would ultimately get the nod?

***

Ever the innovator, Sean Payton devised an unconventional solution to the Saints' 2012 coaching enigma: he enlisted his mentor, Bill Parcells, to potentially assume control of the team for one season.

A certifiable NFL legend, Parcells coached the New York Giants to two Super Bowl titles in eight seasons; led the Patriots to a Super Bowl appearance during the 1996 season; and presided over successful regimes with both the New York Jets and Dallas Cowboys before finally retiring from coaching in 2006.

Parcells groomed Sean Payton for three seasons in Dallas where Payton served as an assistant coach. By all accounts, much of Sean Payton's management style and operational approach derived from his tenure under Parcells. Consequently, it shouldn't have been much of a surprise when Payton approached Parcells about coaching the Saints.

Early in the process, Parcells was amenable to the idea.[46] He said:

> All I can tell you is [Payton] is my friend and that means something to me. I want to be there for him but does that mean stepping in for him and coaching his team if I'm asked? I can't give a definitive answer on that right now because it's all hypothetical.
>
> You know, when I was a young coach, there were people like Chuck Noll, Chuck Knox and Tom Landry who were there for me. I think to honor those guys who helped me, you turn around and pass that legacy on to somebody else and Sean's an example of that. If he needs me and the owner and GM feel the same way, then I'd be a hypocrite if I didn't consider it.

Unsurprisingly, Parcell's mention as a possible replacement generated a wide variety of reactions in the media.

Cleveland Browns' V.P. of Player Personnel Michael Lombardi, then with *The NFL Network,* came out in support[47] of Parcells-to-New Orleans. Lombardi called Payton's idea to seek out Parcells "a great one," and asserted that the Saints' players would never "confuse Parcells for a substitute teacher."

More important for the Saints, Lombardi theorized:

> In this role with New Orleans, Parcells would further the education of all the Saints coaches. He'd teach them how to think like a head coach, how to act like a head coach and most of all, how to be a head coach.
>
> This is the best thing that could happen to rising Saints assistants Pete Carmichael or Aaron Kromer. This experience would make them both better coaches ...
>
> The bar would be raised and the Saints' entire organization would benefit.

Adding Parcells was certainly an intriguing possibility, and one that seemed to be aimed at keeping the Saints as competitive as possible in 2012.

Not all of the members of the NFL media, however, saw it that way. *CBS'* Clark Judge espoused a series of hollow arguments,[48] claiming Parcells had "nothing to prove" (how did Judge know?) and then claimed that Parcells would lack for motivation as head coach in New Orleans (again, how could he possibly know this?).

Judge's flimsy arguments ended with his speculation that Parcells' hiring would be a divisive issue among the existing coaches on the Saints' staff, saying the move would create "internal friction." This was a theory that Judge presented without, apparently, gathering any feedback from Saints' coaches about this possibility.

While Judge was vacuous in his arguments against Parcells' hiring, his colleague Gregg Doyel made the issue a bitingly personal one. Doyel called Payton a "bounty-ignoring monster," "diabolical," and an "arrogant SOB." Doyel further argued that Payton's attempt to lure Parcells was motivated by a desire to enhance "the star power of Sean Payton."

According to Doyel, Payton's motives for soliciting Parcells weren't intended to help the Saints maintain a high level of competitiveness, but rather because Parcells "[hadn't] been good in years" and "would have taken the job with a clear expiration date."

Apparently, Doyel's argument was that Payton's intent was to tank the Saints' 2012 season by hiring an incompetent coach who was no threat to Payton's future in New Orleans. That this was Doyel's argument was absurd enough. But his contention that Bill Parcells, one of the greatest coaches in NFL history, was the incompetent, non-threatening replacement who would ensure Payton's future in New Orleans was downright ignorant.

This was yet another example of a media slant that mostly attempted to exact retribution on Payton for his perceived mistreatment of the media over the years. Much like many of the immediate reactions following Bountygate, these reactions had less to do with the events in question and much more to do with casting Payton and the Saints in a negative light.

Supporting this perception, *CBS'* Mike Freeman called Payton in a March 21st article[49] "the most arrogant man in the sport for the past several years," citing Payton's history -- according to Freeman -- of "[berating] reporters with loads of foul language or [banning] them from covering practice."

***

As the debate over the potential Parcells' hiring raged on in the public domain, and with the succession plan to Sean Payton still uncertain, the Bountygate appeals' process for the punished coaches was nearing. With it, the advent of maybe the strangest twist of the Bountygate saga emerged.

7: "kill the head"

In the early morning hours of April 5th, the events surrounding Bountygate descended into chaos.

A *Yahoo!* report from Mike Silver[50] unveiled the now infamous Gregg Williams' audiotape, recorded in a pregame meeting prior to the Saints' January 2012 playoff game in San Francisco.

During the meeting Williams exhorted the Saints' defense to, among other things:

* "kill the head"

* "lay that fucker (Alex Smith) out"

* turn "[Frank Gore's] head sideways"

* "knock the shit out of" Kendall Hunter

* "affect the head"

* "put a lick" on Kyle Williams to "find out ... about his concussion"

* "find out" if Michael Crabtree would "[become] human when you fucking take out that outside ACL"

Williams' resonating message was "kill the head and the body will die," apparently one of his signature phrases.

At first glance, it appeared the NFL had a smoking gun in their case against the Saints. One of the complicating factors, though, was that this "evidence" was captured by filmmaker Sean Pamphilon -- not the NFL -- who was recording footage for a documentary featuring Steve Gleason.

***

Steve Gleason is a New Orleans' hero, his legend and visage cemented when he blocked a punt minutes into the 2006 Saints-Falcons' game, the first game played in the Superdome after Hurricane Katrina decimated the stadium. The Saints went on to beat their rivals 23-3 that night, setting the stage for a historic 2006 season.

Gleason's block symbolized New Orleans' rebirth -- the city's, its people's, and its football team's -- and it sparked a 2006 season in which the Saints reached the NFC Championship Game for the first time in franchise history.

Gleason became synonymous with New Orleans' civic and cultural resurgence, was loved like a native son and prized as an icon, not just for his achievements on the football field but also for his embrace of and love for the city.

A few years later, when Gleason was cruelly struck with ALS -- an incurable, rapidly progressing, fatal disease -- he enlisted Sean Pamphilon to document portions of his life so that Gleason could preserve a living record for his infant son, Rivers.

With Gleason still a central figure in the Saints' organization in 2011, Pamphilon found himself embedded with the team for much of the 2011 season. When Gleason flew to San Francisco with the team for the January playoff game, he brought Pamphilon along.

Soon after, Pamphilon ended up in the Saints' defensive meeting before the game and recorded Williams' speech. Pamphilon initially kept this footage private for almost four months before breaking rank. The issue at stake was that the footage contractually belonged to Gleason, and not Pamphilon. Nevertheless, Pamphilon eventually decided he controlled the contents and their dissemination.

When it seemed to suit his needs, whatever those might have been, Pamphilon initiated the release of the audiotape against the wishes of Steve Gleason.[51] Fit to apparently betray Gleason and insert himself headfirst into Bountygate, Pamphilon emerged as a mercurial figure of questionable motivation.

In strategically-timed execution that one might consider devious, Mike Silver and Pamphilon released the report and audio on the same morning (Thursday, April 5th) the Saints' coaches, Gregg Williams, and Mickey Loomis were appealing their punishments. News reports from the coaches' appeals were inevitably tied to and tainted by this revealing audio. The established narrative of inarguable, institutional guilt continued to predominate.

Williams' speech only confirmed these preconceptions, and the surfacing of the audio was a fortuitous development for the NFL. For skeptics of the NFL's claims at this point, the Pamphilon audio swayed public sentiment far away from the Saints.

This audio, though, was not a result of the NFL's investigation nor was it a factor in the levying of allegations or dispensing of punishments. It was only a footnote, its contents damning in rhetoric but impotent in practice.

A verifiable piece of information, perhaps overlooked, was the fact that the Saints, in the game following Williams' speech, were penalized not once. No late hits. No roughing the passer penalties. No hands to the face penalties. No hits on defenseless receivers. No illegal chop blocks. Nothing besides a cleanly-played game.

Though the language used and behavior espoused by Gregg Williams was certainly less than beneficent, the fact that it resulted in no penalties incurred or injuries to opponents was equally important to the malicious nature of Williams' rhetoric.

As a result of Williams' exhortations, popular attribution tied the phrase "kill the head and the body will die" directly to Gregg Williams (and by extension, the Saints). This phrase, however, appeared to be a staple of NFL colloquialisms. In fact, the Kansas City Chiefs had a mural of that exact slogan painted in their facility during the tenure of Herm Edwards (2006 – 2008).[52]

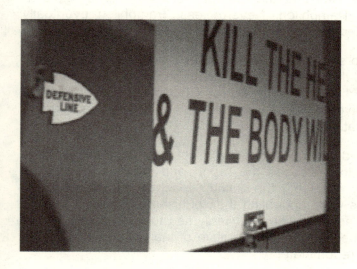

Where Williams employed these words and concepts to motivate, his players never executed his exhortations in a literal sense. The fact that the Saints were not once penalized after being subjected to

Williams' speech lent credence to the fact that his words were motivational and not literal.

Pamphilon, who was on the sideline for the game, said[53] he "[didn't] believe Williams' speech translated into any actual harm to San Francisco players." He also added:

> I was two feet behind the Saints' bench and it looked like they were trying to kill each other every play. But I've watched about 15 NFL games from the sidelines, and I didn't see anything different in that game than I've seen in any other football game. To me, they're all trying to separate guys from the ball and all trying to get big hits that land them on "SportsCenter" – on every play.

This disparity illustrated a central characteristic of the Bountygate allegations: the relationship between the divergent concepts of rhetoric-in-theory and malice-in-practice.

***

Months earlier, on January 24th, 2012, NFL spokesman Greg Aiello noted[54] that "players are accountable for their actions on the field," not their words.

This official league statement was in response to the 2011-'12 NFC Championship Game, in which the New York Giants' Jacquian Williams said of the San Francisco 49ers' Kyle Williams: "The thing is, we knew he had four concussions, so that was our biggest thing, was to take him outta the game."

Aiello continued in his official statement on behalf of the league: "There was no conduct by the Giants of any kind that would suggest an effort to injure Kyle Williams in any way."

Even though the Giants publicly expressed their desire to target a player concussed four times previously -- to "take him out of the game" -- all that mattered to the NFL was what happened on the field. When the NFL found no on-field misconduct on the part of the Giants, they deemed the words meaningless and thus unworthy of discipline.

Yet only a few months later the NFL and Roger Goodell would apply a double standard to the Saints' purported misdeeds, punishing the accused players not for on-field misconduct or injurious deeds, but for a nebulous violation of the "Players' Conduct Policy" that arose from benign motivational tactics and hollow rhetoric.

Not until December of 2012 did the NFL address and parse the significance between rhetoric and malice when Paul Tagliabue, in his ruling on Jonathan Vilma's punishments, stated:[55]

> It is essential to recognize that Vilma is being most severely disciplined for "talk" or speech at a team meeting on the evening before the Saints-Vikings game. He is not being punished for his performance on the field and, indeed, none of the discipline of any player here relates to on-field conduct. No Saints' player was suspended for on-field play by the League ...
>
> The relationship of the discipline for the off-field "talk" and actual on-field conduct must be carefully calibrated and reasonably apportioned. This is a standard grounded in common sense and fairness. It rests also on the competence of NFL officiating and the obligation and ability of the League to closely observe playing field misconduct ...
>
> If one were to punish certain off-field talk in locker rooms, meeting rooms, hotel rooms or elsewhere without applying a rigorous standard that separated real threats or "bounties" from rhetoric and exaggeration, it would open a field of inquiry that would lead nowhere.

In the months before this ruling by Tagliabue, though, Roger Goodell and the NFL would irrevocably railroad the Saints into oblivion mostly based on rhetoric and the claims of a disgruntled, former Saints' employee.

***

In the meantime, by April 10th, Bill Parcells opted to forgo the opportunity to coach the Saints.[56] On April 12th, the Saints named Joe Vitt as their interim coach. According to the Saints and Vitt, this move would keep "Sean Payton's philosophy front and center during this season."[57]

With Vitt set to serve his six-game suspension starting week one of the regular season, the Saints would have to select an interim-interim coach during Vitt's absence. If this pending development wasn't dispiriting to Saints' fans, then it was at least marginally comical. An interim-interim head coach.

The Saints wouldn't make that decision, though, for several months.

As Bountygate was still building steam in its revelations and contentions by mid-April, events in New Orleans outside of the bounty allegations didn't lack for notoriety either.

8: the wiretapping allegations

While Bountygate was swirling, while Drew Brees was negotiating what would ultimately become the largest contract in NFL history, and while *ESPN* was sniffing around the Saints' organization for residual dirt, Saints' owner Tom Benson bought the NBA's New Orleans Hornets on April 13th for a reported $338 million.[58]

It was just another day in one of the strangest years in the history of New Orleans' sports.

In 2002, the Hornets' then-owner George Shinn moved the franchise to New Orleans from Charlotte. The Hornets languished for three seasons as the team attempted to replace the iconic Jazz franchise that had once called New Orleans home. In 2005, with the full brunt of Hurricane Katrina's aftermath upon New Orleans, the Hornets temporarily relocated to Oklahoma City for two seasons.

Upon returning to New Orleans, the Hornets submitted successful seasons in both 2007 and 2008 before a disappointing 2009 season.

By 2010 the Hornets' majority owner George Shinn was in the process of selling the team to minority owner Gary Chouest,[59] but when that deal failed to materialize, the NBA stepped in and purchased the Hornets to stabilize the franchise and ensure its future in New Orleans.[60]

As the NBA sought an owner committed to New Orleans for the long term, none better came to mind than Benson. By the time his Saints' franchise was knee-deep in turmoil, Benson was finalizing the Hornets' purchase.

Though it was a temporarily pleasant distraction for New Orleans and Saints' fans, it paled in comparison to the bombshell that *ESPN* dropped ten days later on April 23rd.

***

Reporting for *ESPN's* "Outside the Lines," John Barr alleged the Saints illegally eavesdropped on opponents. More specifically, Barr contended the Saints placed electronic devices and wiretaps in the Superdome that enabled them to monitor the communications of their opponents during the 2002 - 2004 seasons.

Barr's report stated:[61]

> The U.S. Attorney's Office in the Eastern District of Louisiana was told Friday that New Orleans Saints general manager Mickey Loomis had an electronic device in his Superdome suite that had been secretly re-wired to enable him to eavesdrop on visiting coaching staffs for nearly three NFL seasons, "Outside the Lines" has learned.
>
> Sources familiar with Saints game-day operations told "Outside the Lines" that Loomis, who faces an eight-game suspension from the NFL for his role in the recent bounty scandal, had the ability to secretly listen for most of the 2002 season, his first as general manager of the Saints, and all of the 2003 and 2004 seasons. The sources spoke with "Outside the Lines" under the condition of anonymity because of fear of reprisals from members of the Saints organization.

These were damning criminal allegations, the truth of which remained unknown, but on the heels of Bountygate, they exacerbated the chaos and hysteria enveloping the Saints.

The report went on to allege:

> Sources told "Outside the Lines" the listening device was first installed in the general manager's suite in 2000, when Loomis' predecessor, Randy Mueller, served as Saints GM. At that time, according to sources, Mueller had the ability to use the device to monitor only the game-day communications of the Saints' coaching staff, not the opposing coaches. Mueller, now a senior executive with the San Diego Chargers (he also was an ESPN.com NFL analyst from 2002 to '05), declined to comment when contacted by "Outside the Lines."
>
> After the transition from Mueller to Loomis, the electronic device was re-wired to listen only to opposing coaches and could no longer be used to listen to any game-day communications between members of the Saints' coaching staff, one source said.
>
> "There was a switch, and the switch accessed offense and defense," said the source. "When Randy was there, it was the Saints offense or defense, and when Mickey was there it changed over so it was the visiting offense or defense," the source said.

The timing of these allegations -- not yet two months after Bountygate -- undermined the report's veracity, considering these were decade-old accusations. Nearly ten years after the purported events, "anonymous sources" apparently decided to step forward and inform the U.S. District Attorney of this allegation. This event reeked of ulterior motive.

Mostly, it seemed like this report was a shot in the dark by *ESPN* to manufacture a timely headline that perpetuated the budding narrative that the Saints were a rogue organization.

Barr's report, however, presented no definitive evidence or conclusions, just vague intimations from unknown sources. Instead of identifying a specific source, Barr cited a "[source] familiar with Saints game-day operations." This could be any number of persons, not necessarily someone intimately familiar with the electronic communications in the Superdome.

A day after the report surfaced, Saints' audio engineer Robert Carroll went on the record to cast doubt on Barr's report. According to Carroll, his first reaction to the story was that "this is crazy; this is ridiculous."[62] Would Carroll have known about the setup had it existed? "Absolutely, without question," he said. He added: "I've spent too many hours in that Superdome not to think I would have seen something."

Carroll wasn't the only person connected to the Saints who quickly refuted the report.

Cortez Kennedy, who worked as an advisor to the team under Loomis, said: "This is completely false. I have sat with Mickey for years, for multiple games and I can say that when Mickey gets up to go walk around during breaks or halftime, I put his earpiece in ... it is WWL-AM radio. ... I know this, because I have heard. Plain and simple."[63]

Saints' director of college scouting Rick Reiprish, who often sat next to Loomis when the misdeeds were alleged to have occurred said: "This is completely untrue, there was never any kind of electronic device to listen in on any other booths, and this is certainly not something Mickey Loomis would engage in."[64]

Former Saints' director of player personnel (2002) Rick Mueller said "there is no way this happened."[65]

Even included in *ESPN's* original report were refutations from former Saints' coaches Jim Haslett and Rick Venturi. While the actuality of the listening device itself remained in question, John Barr made sure to note that "'Outside the Lines' could not determine for certain whether Loomis ever made use of the electronic setup."

On the surface the report seemed damning. But when one peeled back the layers, it seemed like a collection of silly conjecture. Contrasted to the anonymous sources -- capacities unknown, motives undetermined, credibility in question -- were a litany of Saints' insiders immediately going on the record to refute the allegations. Further, *ESPN* admitted that there was no evidence this supposed device, even if it did exist, was ever actually used.

Nonetheless the issuing of this report contributed to an encompassing doom facing the Saints. It generated headlines and web clicks for *ESPN*, and it built upon the nefarious perception of the Saints.

Soon after *ESPN* released their report, the FBI and Louisiana State Police commenced an investigation. Concurrently, Mickey Loomis held a press conference on April 26th to clear his name. Of the allegations Loomis said: "I'm angry about it, frankly. It's not true. I have a clear conscience." More comprehensively, Loomis stated in unequivocal terms:[66]

> Regarding the eavesdropping allegations: in my 28 or 29 years in the NFL, I have never listened to an opposing team's communication. I have never asked for the capability to listen to an opposing team's communications. I have never inquired as to the possibility of listening in on an opposing team's communications. I've never been aware of any capability to listen in on an opposing team's communications at the Superdome or at any NFL stadium.

Loomis said he welcomed an investigation by the FBI and LA. State Police because he knew "it didn't happen." This corroborated the Saints' team statement that the accusations were "1000% false."[67]

***

By August 13th the Louisiana State Police, working in conjunction with the FBI, completed their investigation into the wiretapping matter.

They found no evidence supporting *ESPN's* allegations. In a press conference announcing the investigation's results, State Police Col.

Mike Edmondson stated:[68] "We found no corroborating evidence that Mickey Loomis or anybody in the Saints was engaged in wiretapping or eavesdropping."

***

With the NFL soon to release their sanctions to the players allegedly involved in Bountygate in early May, the Saints were faced with yet another distraction from the wiretapping accusations. Instead of subsiding, the dramatics of 2012 continued to build and there was seemingly no end in sight.

And as the dynamics of Bountygate continued to increase in their complexity, another eye-opening twist was about to surface.

9: conduct detrimental

One day after Mickey Loomis proclaimed his innocence over the wiretapping allegations and one day after the first round of the 2012 NFL draft, Joe Hummel announced his resignation from his job.[69]

Who was Joe Hummel? He was the NFL's Director of Investigations, the man who was conducting the Saints' bounty investigation.

According to NFL spokesman Greg Aiello, Hummel was departing within a month for a "senior security position at a large company ... a big opportunity."[70]

Once again, the timing of the event raised questions. First, the NFL leaked the news of Hummel's resignation on a Friday afternoon (April 27th) while the football universe both analyzed the results of the draft's first round and anticipated the second round's commencement later that night. With all of the other NFL activity, the Hummel announcement didn't rate to register much attention.

It seemed, mostly, like the NFL was intentionally trying to bury the story at a time when NFL fans would be less likely to notice. For those paying attention, this was an important development in the bounty saga: the Director of Investigations, in the midst of an ongoing inquiry, abruptly announcing his resignation.

More important, the players involved with Bountygate were still waiting to learn their punishments from Roger Goodell. Hummel's resignation at this juncture in the process perhaps reflected an investigation in disarray, especially because the NFL had delayed the issuance of player penalties with little explanation or transparency. If the NFL was continuing to investigate (in early April, they called it an "ongoing investigation"[71]), then it seemed important to have an investigator on the job who didn't already have one foot out of the door.

By April 27th, it had been over a month since the NFL announced punishments to the coaches and Saints' organization. The fact that the NFL was continuing to investigate was mildly disturbing, considering that the coaches and team had already been disciplined. If there was exculpatory evidence out there, it would be of no use to the coaches at this point.

At any rate, the longer the delay in player punishments, the more damage to the Saints. Without knowing who would be punished and to what extent, the Saints were unable to properly develop a contingency plan. This plan would involve signing free agents, selecting replacements via the NFL draft, shuffling position assignments, etc. If the NFL was committed to being responsible to the Saints (and by extension, the competitive integrity of the league) while this process unfolded, an expedited resolution seemed fair.

But for some reason, the NFL was dragging its feet on announcing player punishments. If the players had "enthusiastically embraced" the program (as Goodell was fond of saying), if the NFL had collected years' worth of damning evidence, then why wasn't a verdict yet in?

Perhaps the NFL was getting its ducks in a row in anticipation of a protracted battle with the NFLPA. Or maybe the NFL's evidence wasn't quite as strong as they publicly proclaimed it to be, and they were attempting to solidify their case before proceeding against the players and their union.

Either way, weeks earlier (April 2nd), Roger Goodell said:[72] "I think we all need to move forward" in reference to handing down player suspensions. Equally important, Goodell stated that he was awaiting a "recommendation from [the NFLPA]" in order to determine suitable player sanctions. Yet almost a month after these statements, nothing had yet materialized.

Why so?

On April 16th, in reference to the bounty allegations, the NFL Players' Association (NFLPA) made public this critical information: "To date, the NFL has not provided the NFLPA with detailed evidence of the existence of such a program."[73]

While Goodell publicly stated that he wanted the NFLPA's input on player punishments, he had failed to -- according to the NFLPA -- provide them with any evidence supporting his allegations. And that was presumably hindering the continuation of the process.

Additionally, Drew Brees had publicly bolstered the NFLPA's claim when he said, after a meeting of NFL and NFLPA representatives on April 16th, "we didn't get any meaningful evidence, or any meaningful truth or facts."[74]

By April 24th, Roger Goodell had pivoted from his April 2nd assertion that he was waiting for NFLPA input before dispensing punishments. In an interview with the *NFL Network's* Rich Eisen, Goodell, perhaps growing frustrated with the NFLPA's desire to see evidence before reaching a verdict, said: "I am not necessarily looking for [the NFLPA's] recommendation on discipline."[75]

Suddenly Goodell had changed his mind over the NFLPA's role in shaping player punishments, and threatened to unilaterally move forward. All signs pointed to the NFLPA's request to see evidence as the source of Goodell's pivot.

Three days later when Joe Hummel resigned, the NFL's position suddenly appeared a bit more precarious than they had previously presented with their airtight claims of "forensic experts" and 50,000 pages of documentation.

By the end of April, there were mounting public refutations from Saints' players, employees, and the NFLPA; a failure by the NFL to disclose evidence to anyone involved; an unexplained delay in dispensing player punishments; and Joe Hummel's abrupt resignation.

Murky were the waters.

***

On May 2nd, the NFL issued sanctions to four players.[76] In summary, the punishments were:

1.) Scott Fujita: three game suspension without pay, effective week one of the regular season

The NFL's official statement asserted: "The record established that Fujita, a linebacker, pledged a significant amount of money to the prohibited pay-for-performance/bounty pool …"

2.) Anthony Hargrove: eight game suspension without pay, effective week one of the regular season

In its official statement, the NFL claimed "Hargrove submitted a signed declaration to the league that established not only the existence of the program at the Saints, but also that he knew about and participated in it."

In addition to that, they claimed "Hargrove told at least one player on another team that Vikings quarterback Brett Favre was a target of a large bounty during the NFC Championship Game in January of 2010." Finally, the NFL punished Hargrove for "actively [obstructing] the league's 2010 investigation into the program by being untruthful to investigators."

3.) Will Smith: four game suspension without pay, effective week one of the regular season

According to the league's investigation, Smith "assisted Saints defensive coordinator Gregg Williams in establishing and funding the program during a period in which he was a captain and leader of the defensive unit."

4.) Jonathan Vilma: suspended without pay for the entire 2012 season, effective immediately

The NFL claimed Vilma "assisted coach Williams in establishing and funding the program." More gravely, the NFL punished Vilma for "[offering] a specific bounty -- $10,000 in cash -- to any player who knocked Arizona quarterback Kurt Warner out of the 2009 divisional playoff game and later pledged the same amount to anyone who knocked Minnesota quarterback Brett Favre out of the 2009 NFC Championship Game the following week."

The NFL's statement further asserted that "the evidence conclusively demonstrated that from 2009 - 2011 Saints players of their own accord pledged significant amounts of their own money toward bounties." Outside of the alleged bounties on Warner and Favre during the 2009 season, the NFL failed to identify any other opponents targeted by bounties when sanctioning the players in May. At the same time the NFL continued to claim "bounties" during three seasons, going so far as to mention it in this statement.

If the Saints targeted opponents for injury in 2010 and 2011, who were those targets? If they existed, why were they not worthy of mention here? Were Saints' players not punished for offering bounties on these mystery players?

Lastly, and perhaps most relevant of all, the NFL punished the players for "conduct detrimental to the NFL," a violation of the Player's Conduct Policy which governed off-field issues.

This distinction, as mentioned earlier, was integral to the process and revealing of the reality of the allegations. The NFL didn't discipline the players for any on-field misconduct. By punishing the players for "conduct detrimental," the NFL tacitly admitted that the players never participated in injurious, malicious activity on the field. Had they, the NFL certainly would have identified the specific misdeeds and then levied punishment for them.

Instead, the NFL punished players under the auspices of a vague, non-playing related statute that allowed Roger Goodell, by virtue of the league's collective bargaining agreement, to solely control the process of punishments and appeals. In short, this enabled Goodell to produce an outcome that he alone deemed appropriate.

Through this strategy, combined with his failure to share evidence with the accused parties, Goodell was presiding over a flawed, cynical episode that presumably had only one result in mind: punishing the Saints and the players allegedly involved at any cost.

By all appearances Goodell was intent on sending a message and that end justified his means, no matter how unjust. During a May 31st press conference Goodell said his Bountygate "actions speak very loudly."[77] And this, apparently, was his overarching goal: to send a very loud message, truth be damned.

Most of the claims behind these player punishments, as we'd eventually learn, were unreliable or proven false. But in the meantime, the accused players found themselves in the midst of an opaque, corrupt process that tarnished their reputations and threatened their careers.

Unsurprisingly, the NFLPA reacted swiftly to these punishments. Their May 2nd statement read:[78]

> After seeing the NFL's decision letters, the NFLPA has still not received any detailed or specific evidence from the league of these specific players' involvement in an alleged pay-to-injure program. We have made it clear that punishment without evidence is not fair. We have spoken with our players and their representatives and we will vigorously protect and pursue all options on their behalf.

This response was a reiteration of previous statements -- that the NFL repeatedly failed to provide the NFLPA, the one entity that could ensure some semblance of a fair process, with any evidence of wrongdoing.

No matter, Roger Goodell lobbed accusations, levied sanctions, and expected everyone involved to take his word for it, to assume his truthfulness and good intention.

Jonathan Vilma responded on the day the NFL announced their punishments. He said:[79]

> I am shocked and extremely disappointed by the NFL's decision to suspend me for the 2012 season. Commissioner Roger Goodell has refused to share any of the supposed evidence he claims supports this unprecedented punishment. The reason is clear: I never paid, or intended to pay, $10,000, or any amount of money, to any player for knocking Kurt Warner, Brett Favre or any other player, out of the 2009 divisional playoff game, 2010 NFC championship game, or any other game.
>
> I never set out to intentionally hurt any player and never enticed any teammate to intentionally hurt another player. I also never put any money into a bounty pool or helped to create a bounty pool intended to pay out money for injuring other players. I have always conducted myself in a professional and proud manner. I intend to fight this injustice, to defend my reputation, to stand up for my team and my profession, and to send a clear signal to the commissioner that the process has failed, to the detriment of me, my teammates, the New Orleans Saints and the game.

Vilma's statement directly and forcefully rebutted the league's contentions. He denied offering a bounty at any time on any opponent, while also refuting the claim that he helped establish a bounty program. This challenge from Vilma, this "clear signal," hinted at a larger future fight.

On the same day, Will Smith released a statement in which he said:[80]

> I am disappointed the NFL has punished me with a four game suspension. I have never in my career, nor as a Captain asked others, to intentionally target and hurt specific opposing players. I was in no way involved in establishing or assisting Gregg Williams with implementing a bounty program. The accusations made against me are completely and one-hundred percent false, and I plan to appeal the decision along with the help of the NFL Players Association.

> Through this entire process, the NFL never notified me of what I was being accused of, nor presented me with any evidence or reasoning for this decision. I am interested in discovering who is making these specific and false accusations, and as well as why a decision was made without speaking with me and giving me the opportunity to review the facts. I am going to work with my union to clear my name and returning to the game I love and respect. Thank you to our fans for the continued support.

Besides calling the accusation "one hundred percent false," Smith's statement further reiterated the overtly corrupt process to which the players were subjected.

Smith said he was "never notified of what [he] was being accused of" nor was he ever presented "with any evidence." Moreover, Smith noted that a person -- identity in question -- had levied "false accusations"; further, the NFL failed to present this accuser for cross examination.

The picture that emerged was of a one-sided nature: the NFL was alleging a variety of damning claims that the players fiercely contested, while refusing to share evidence and further shielding the identity of their primary source.

If Roger Goodell's goal was a predetermined outcome of guilt, then his preferred method of railroading the players was achieving that end.

But it wouldn't last.

***

On May 3rd, a day after the NFL announced the punishments and a day after the NFLPA and players responded with clear denials, the NFL trotted out Mary Jo White to bolster their position.

White is a former U.S. District Attorney, the current chair of litigation at a major New York law firm, and recent nominee as Chairwoman of the Securities and Exchange Commission. The NFL retained White to provide an "independent review" of the league's evidence. When questioned over her role in the process, White said on May 3rd: "In terms of 'am I independent?', the answer is yes I am."[81]

Though the NFL positioned White as an "independent" third party, that characterization was mildly confusing -- if not wholly disingenuous --

considering the NFL was paying her to review evidence, while at the same time refusing to share that evidence with anyone else. That White would later lead the NFL's legal team during the Bountygate appeals' process was also noteworthy: an individual first presented as a neutral evaluator was in reality in concert with the NFL.

How someone with a clear motive (and paycheck) for advancing the NFL's interests in the bounty case could be "independent" or objective is anyone's guess.

At any rate, the NFL provided White to the media for a conference call on May 3rd. The nature of this call was for White to present her review of the evidence, and to respond to the denials from the NFLPA and the players involved.

White's primary message, in relation to the veracity of the charges and evidence, was this: "It isn't the case where you should have any concerns of reliability in this information."[82] Her message seemed to be "take our word for it."

White noted several times that "multiple, independent sources" corroborated the allegations without noting who these sources were. When questioned about the players' request to review the evidence, face their accusers and challenge their allegations, White laughably called that seemingly fundamental right "a red herring issue." Moreover, White characterized the NFL's process as "thorough, fair, and robust," even though the NFL steadfastly refused to both share the source evidence and allow the accused to face their accusers.

By the NFL's standards, this was a "fair" process when it seemed anything but.

Mike Florio of *Pro Football Talk*, a former attorney turned NFL newsman, said this[83] of the developments from White's media call:

> ... the thing that struck me as most significant is the fact that the NFL hasn't, and possibly won't, give the players full information regarding the persons who have accused them of participating in a bounty program ... it appears that, for now, only general summaries and characterizations of the information have been provided to the NFLPA. If the players are going to mount any type of a meaningful defense, that's not good enough.

Florio wasn't alone on this point. Enter Peter Ginsberg, Jonathan Vilma's attorney.

Responding to the accusations, punishments, and Mary Jo White's statements, Ginsberg said this[84] in an interview on *WWL Radio*:

> What the commissioner has said publicly, the accusations and allegations against Jonathan are not true. They are simply not accurate.
>
> The fact that we haven't received a single piece of evidence from the commissioner ... makes the whole process suspect ... This is not the first time we have asked them for the evidence.
>
> ... the commissioner's office and the commissioner's outside counsel have discernibly misrepresented even the information that the commissioner has gathered ... It really puts into perspective the kangaroo court that Jonathan and the others have been subjected to. I can't think of any other forum in the United States where this kind of abusive process is permitted.
>
> The evidence is not what the commissioner says it is. At the end of the day, I think all of you will come to the conclusion that what the commissioner has been accusing Jonathan and the others of doing is not correct. It's not accurate.

If it wasn't previously clear that a battle between the accused players and the NFL was imminent, it certainly was now. Ginsberg openly and directly derided the NFL's methods, calling it an "abusive process." He painted their charges as "not true" and "not accurate." He accused them of misrepresenting the truth and subjecting the players to a "kangaroo court."

At the same, the NFLPA initiated action[85] that challenged Goodell's authority on this issue. In short, they accused Goodell of "[violating] the [league's] duty of fairness to the players" and also "[failing] to [disclose] sufficient evidence of violations."

Specifically the NFLPA filed a System Arbitration that challenged Goodell's jurisdiction on the matter. They also filed a Non-Injury Grievance that stipulated the NFL was prohibited from punishing players for conduct that allegedly occurred prior to the signing of the most recent collective bargaining agreement (August 4, 2011).[86]

The first of these was a procedural challenge designed to shift control of the process from Goodell to a third party.

Ultimately, the appeals' process would work in favor of the players. But that was many months away, after many different iterations and appellate processes.

In the meantime, the legal battle was officially underway. On May 17th, Jonathan Vilma sued Roger Goodell for defamation in federal court. Specifically, Vilma's suit "[contended] Goodell lied about Vilma when making public statements about Vilma's role in the alleged bounty program."[87]

Vilma, assuredly, was intent on clearing his name.

***

With the legal battles commenced and with the players' appeals looming in the next two months, Drew Brees and the Saints continued to negotiate a new contract. In the two months since the Saints had applied the franchise tag to Brees, the two parties had failed to agree on the parameters of a deal. The negotiations, by all accounts, were stalled without a resolution in sight.

With that in mind, Brees set out to make a bit of history for the first time in 2012.

10: challenging the franchise tag designation

In late May, Drew Brees sought arbitration[88] to determine whether his franchise tag designation by the Saints was interpreted (under the league's collective bargaining agreement) as the first or second time he'd been assigned the "tag" during his career.

Clarifying this designation was important because it would influence negotiating baselines, and affect the ultimate value of the new contract Brees would sign. According to the collective bargaining agreement that governed the designation, "tagged" players were guaranteed certain salary benchmarks. Further, the more times a team tags a player, the more money they must guarantee him.

The source of contention here was determining whether Brees was considered tagged for the first time or the second. Was the language in the CBA specific to the player's tenure with one team at a time? Or was it broadly applied to a player's entire career, regardless of how many teams he played for and was tagged by?

This was critical because in 2005, the San Diego Chargers applied the franchise tag to Brees. During that season, Brees played under a one-year contract at salary guaranteed by the tag. In the last game of 2005, Brees suffered a near catastrophic injury to his shoulder and faced the prospect of never playing again.

As we know, Brees recovered just fine. But by playing in 2005 under the tag, a designation that Brees had no control over, Brees was unable to play under the security of a long-term contract that protected his future, especially in the case of injury. By being tagged, Brees was also unable to negotiate with and potentially play for any other team. He was boxed in to playing under a one-year deal because the Chargers were unwilling, at that time, to renegotiate a long-term deal with him. While that was an inescapable reality, it was also a limiting designation.

By the end of 2011 when Brees' six-year deal with the Saints expired, the Saints tagged Brees. Though this was the first time the Saints had tagged him, it was the second time Brees had been tagged in his career. Clearly, Brees was adamant about refusing to play (again) under the insecurity of a one-year contract.

In fact, Brees said:[89] "I've played under the franchise tag before, back in 2005, and that ended with 13 anchors in my right shoulder and a 25 percent chance of playing football again. That didn't work out too well for me. I've talked to the Saints about this many times. They definitely know my desire to have a long-term deal."

As Brees steadfastly refused to sign a one-year deal, the end result was either Brees signing a long-term contract or Brees sitting out the 2012 season. And while the Saints were committed to signing Brees for the long haul, his new contract would almost certainly be the richest in NFL history. That alone presented obstacles. With Brees having substantially outplayed his previous contract -- one that paid him in line with being a league-average quarterback -- Brees would seek a precedent-setting contract that compensated him for being underpaid during the years' prior.

Though that seemed to be the case, the Saints' job was to pay Brees in line with his current and future value. The negotiations were far from simple. When more than two months passed without a new deal being completed, Brees decided to clarify his franchise tag status and, by extension, clarify his value. The logic was that this determination would facilitate the completion of a contract.

But that wasn't the only purpose in seeking clarification. This determination would also set a precedent for NFL players going forward. If the arbitrator ruled that the franchise tag language in the CBA broadly applied to a player's entire career, and was thus not specific to a player's tenure with one team at a time, the franchise tag designation would be weakened. For the players, this would be a beneficial ruling.

How so? Again, the more times a player is assigned the tag, the more guaranteed money he is owed under the one-year contracts that come with the franchise tag. The more times a player receives the tag, then, the less incentive teams have in applying it. Instead, a longer-term contract will generally be more mutually beneficial.

NFL players often view the franchise tag with disdain because it minimizes their options (i.e., negotiating with other teams) and limits their long-term security. Any legal precedent that would discourage teams from applying the franchise tag would be a victory for the players.

And this is what Brees sought to do, ideally: limit the effectiveness of the inherently-limiting franchise tag designation. A ruling in his favor would not only enhance his contract value, it would potentially benefit every NFL player going forward.

By May 29th when Brees sought clarification on this issue, time was of the essence. The deadline for Brees and the Saints to complete a long-term contract was July 16th. If a deal wasn't in place by then, Brees would either have to play under a one-year contract as designated by his franchise tag status, or sit out the entire year. As Brees said repeatedly, he would not play under a one-year deal.

At this point, it was do (long-term deal) or die (sit out).

On July 3rd, System Arbitrator Stephen Burbank ruled in Brees' favor. He determined that this was Brees' second designation under the tag. The *Associated Press'* Brett Martel reported:[90]

> Burbank ... ruled that while the NFL's CBA has some ambiguity on the matter, it is clear that the overarching purpose of the language regarding multiple franchise tags is meant to protect players from being denied their rights to free agency for an undue length of their careers.

Further, the NFLPA responded by saying:[91] "This ruling will help all franchise players in the future. We are very happy that Drew Brees has clarification on this matter, and we hope that it facilitates a successful negotiation for Drew and the Saints."

In a season of unprecedented developments, Brees set a precedent of his own. Not only was this a victory for him, it was also a victory for his union and a benefit to his colleagues going forward.

Soon after, on July 13th, Drew Brees, the Saints, and their fans received a much-needed dose of good news: Brees agreed to a $100 million, five-year contract[92] that paid him a signing bonus of $40 million and guaranteed him $60 million over the contract's first three years.

Equally important, Brees would be present for training camp. During a traumatic offseason, the Saints badly needed Brees' presence and leadership. Now finally they would have it.

***

While Brees was setting in motion a process to resolve his contract quagmire, May and June brought the public leaking of information purporting to be evidence in the Bountygate case.

Mischaracterizations, distortions, and falsehoods defined this subject material. With the players' appeals set for mid June, the public would soon get its first glimpse at the source evidence the NFL used in dispensing punishments.

It was far from damning.

11: examining the bountygate evidence

The NFL scheduled the players' first appeal of their punishments for June 18th. As governed by the league's collective bargaining agreement (CBA), Roger Goodell -- the person who dispensed the original punishments -- presided over the appeals' process as well.

After Roger Goodell punished the four players involved, but before the appeals started, portions of the NFL's Bountygate evidence intermittently found its way into the public domain.

More completely, complying with a CBA mandate that compelled Goodell to furnish an official set of evidence to the players three days prior to their appeals, the NFL released 200 pages of evidence on Monday, June 15th.

With this official release from the NFL and the variety of leaked information already available, something resembling a full body of evidence emerged.

What follows here (and partly in the subsequent chapter) is an analysis of many of the items considered "evidence," their public characterizations, their flaws, and their ultimate realities.

1.) Anthony Hargrove's "Declaration"

When the NFL claimed in its punishment of Anthony Hargrove that[93] "Hargrove submitted a signed declaration to the league that established not only the existence of the program at the Saints, but also that he knew about and participated in it," they made a patently false statement.

Doubling down, the NFL had counsel Mary Jo White perpetuate this falsehood on May 3rd when she said:[94]

> There hasn't been any denial of the existence of that program. One of the Saints players (current Packers DE Anthony Hargrove) who was disciplined yesterday actually submitted a declaration in which he acknowledged that the program existed, acknowledged his participation and admitted that he lied to the NFL investigators in 2010.

This statement from Mary Jo White was an outright lie. Four days later (May 7th), Hargrove's actual declaration[95] leaked. In it, he testified that he "repeatedly denied knowledge of any bounty or bounty program." Where White and the NFL said Hargrove "acknowledged that a program existed," Hargrove in actuality denied that it existed.

For whatever reason, White wholly misrepresented Hargrove's testimony even after having (apparently) read his declaration.

More specifically, Hargrove said this in his declaration:

> The NFL Security personnel asked me if there had been a bounty on Brett Favre in the NFC Championship game, and as instructed by Coach Williams and Coach Vitt, I denied all knowledge of a bounty or bounty program.
>
> The NFL Security personnel then asked several questions about whether there was a bounty program, whether Saints' players contributed money to a bounty pool, and whether I had ever received bounty money. In response to these questions, I followed the clear directions I had received from Coach Williams and Coach Vitt, and I repeatedly denied knowledge of any bounty or bounty program.

It's fair to perceive Hargrove's testimony with varied interpretations. But the verifiable, factual content of his testimony -- his "repeatedly [denying] knowledge of any bounty or bounty program" -- directly refuted the NFL's public claim that Hargrove "established the existence of the program ... and participated in it."

This was the NFL's first misrepresentation, of four, attributed to Hargrove.

This claim was a key tenet in Hargrove's punishment, and its truth was in sharp dispute. On May 9th, Hargrove said the NFL "grossly mischaracterized [his] words."[96]

Equally significant, Hargrove submitted this declaration on April 13th, 2012. This was three weeks *after* the NFL disciplined the coaches. Official documentation of Hargrove's testimony was, apparently, of little importance prior to sanctioning the coaches. In fact, the NFLPA -- not the NFL -- produced this declaration. Prior to the declaration's existence, the NFL simply claimed Hargrove's testimony was what they wanted it to be. Even after being aware of what Hargrove's declaration factually stated, the NFL still continued to falsify Hargrove's words.

When this document leaked publicly, it was clear the NFL had falsely attributed testimony to Hargrove in order to fit their claims.

2.) "Pay me my money"

First reported by Peter King in his aforementioned May 12th "Bounty Culture" article (titled *"Way Out of Bounds"*) in *Sports Illustrated*, King intimated that NFL microphones captured Anthony Hargrove demanding payment for a bounty on Brett Favre. Here's how King positioned it without directly accusing Hargrove:[97]

> Favre suffered a badly sprained left ankle on that play and had to be helped off the field. On the New Orleans sideline, Hargrove excitedly slapped hands with teammates, saying, "Favre is out of the game! Favre is done! Favre is done!"
>
> An on-field microphone directed toward the sideline caught an unidentified defender saying, "Pay me my money!"

This was the first mention of Hargrove's possible connection to the alleged Favre bounty, and King presumably learned of this from his NFL sources prior to penning the article early in the Bountygate timeline.

By Monday, June 18th the NFL directly accused Hargrove of making this statement,[98] only the words attributed to Hargrove had changed. Now the NFL claimed Hargrove said "Bobby, give me my money." "Bobby" apparently referenced then Saints' defensive end Bobby McCray, an individual who wasn't implicated in or indicted for any related Bountygate transgression.

For whatever reason, either the NFL or Peter King mistook or misheard what Hargrove supposedly said. If that wasn't the case, then perhaps the audio wasn't clear enough to discern what was in fact said. Either way, there were conflicting reports on what Hargrove supposedly said.

Hargrove, though, adamantly denied making the statement. On Tuesday June 19th, speaking in front of NFL headquarters in New York, Hargrove said:

> The NFL has a sideline shot of our defense gathered around Joe Vitt discussing what we might should expect if the backup quarterback comes into the game. It shows me off to the side with some of our other defensive linemen on the bench with their

backs to the camera. The final snippet has an arrow pointed at me with the caption indicating that I had said, "give me my money."

Here's the problem with that. It wasn't me. That's right. The NFL got their evidence all wrong. In their rush to convict me, they made a very serious error. Is it intentional? I don't know. But one thing I do know with absolute certainty...it...was...not...me!

Like I said, lean in closer, look closer, listen closer. It is not my voice. Anyone who knows me well knows that it is not me. But the NFL does not know me well. They simply make assumptions.

It's fair to note here that Hargrove didn't deny that those words were said; he only denied saying them. Regardless, for the second time in two months, the NFL misrepresented Hargrove's role in an effort to fortify their bounty case. This activity by the NFL -- this inability to gather basic facts, this failure to relay substantiated truth -- continued to reveal an investigation riddled with flaws.

As for Hargrove, this wasn't the last time the NFL would falsely accuse him.

3.) The Jimmy Kennedy Connection

When the NFL issued its statement on player discipline, they cited that[99] "Hargrove told at least one player on another team that Vikings quarterback Brett Favre was a target of a large bounty during the NFC Championship Game in January of 2010." Eventually, the public learned this "player on another team" was the Vikings' Jimmy Kennedy.

Specifically, the NFL said this about Kennedy's involvement in an October 9th, 2012 memo:[100]

> In subsequent discussions, Coach Childress said that a Vikings player, Jimmy Kennedy, had told him that the Saints defensive unit had offered a $10,000 bounty on Mr. Favre and that Mr. Kennedy had identified Anthony Hargrove, then a defensive player for the Saints, as the source of his information ...
>
> Our office promptly investigated this matter. We interviewed Coach Childress and Mr. Kennedy.

Only Kennedy denied this claim soon after. Kennedy accused the NFL of distributing "blatant lies about [him]."[101] He continued, saying this:

> Coach Childress approached me and asked me if I knew anything about such an allegation, and I told him the truth: I did not. I had no knowledge of any such alleged bounty.
>
> It simply never happened. I never discussed an alleged bounty with Anthony Hargrove before, during or after the NFC Championship Game. The only discussion I have had with Anthony about the alleged bounty occurred when we recently spoke about the NFL's egregiously flawed and unjust investigation and proceeding.

About the allegation that the NFL interviewed him, Kennedy took to Twitter to deny that accusation. He said:[102]

> I NEVER interviewed with anyone from #NFL, No NFL Security, Not Goodell, NO ONE!

Again, this was an instance of the NFL claiming something in a memo that supported their version of events that was later vehemently disputed by the implicated party.

Was the NFL lying about Kennedy's involvement? Did they interview him or not? If Kennedy was so adamant that this didn't happen, then why did the NFL say it did?

4.) Hargrove obstructs the NFL's investigation

On May 2nd, the NFL punished Hargrove for "actively [obstructing] the league's 2010 investigation into the program by being untruthful to investigators."[103]

Aside from this statement, the NFL provided no additional details as to how Hargrove obstructed their investigation. They simply said he did without explaining how he was untruthful. Additionally, Paul Tagliabue said in his December 11th ruling that Hargrove "contributed to the obstruction of the investigation by providing denials as instructed by his coaches."[104]

Simply because Hargrove denied the existence of a bounty program, though, did not make those denials inherently untruthful.

More relevant, Tagliabue later said this in his final ruling on Anthony Hargrove:[105]

> As a further complication, it is unclear exactly what NFL investigators asked Hargrove regarding the Program or any other alleged program and, thus, unclear whether he lied about the Program or the fact that it included cart-offs and knockouts. There is evidence in the appeals record that NFL investigators may not have asked Hargrove whether the Saints employed any particular program.

Though Tagliabue appeared to support Roger Goodell's initial finding that Hargrove obstructed the league, he clearly stated that it was "unclear whether [Hargrove] lied" when questioned by league investigators. Further, Tagliabue revealed that there was evidence that indicated NFL investigators may not have even asked Hargrove about a bounty program.

No matter, Goodell and the NFL still concluded that Hargrove obstructed their investigation and punished him as a result. Even without knowing what questions NFL investigators presented to Hargrove, Goodell nevertheless accused Hargrove of lying.

This act by Roger Goodell was stark in its cynicism: it revealed that the substance of Hargrove's meeting with NFL investigators was irrelevant. More absurdly, on the whole, is that the NFL ultimately claimed that Hargrove both obstructed their investigation, and admitted to the existence of a bounty program. How Hargrove's actions were simultaneously an admission *and* an obstruction defied the principles of rudimentary logic.

Most important, this sequence indicated a predetermined outcome of guilt regardless of what the record actually revealed. And it again called into question the integrity of the league's investigation and the veracity of their accusations.

A further question to consider is Anthony Hargrove's central role in the NFL's case. Why did the NFL, in attempting to publicly "sell" their version of events, choose to four times misrepresent allegations connected to Hargrove? And why was Anthony Hargrove the only Saints' player interviewed by the NFL during their investigation?

Did the NFL attempt to coerce Hargrove's assent because he twice violated the NFL's substance abuse policy?[106] Did they assume he'd fear for his career prospects if he refuted their claims, and would thus be more likely to go along with the accusations?

5.) The Mike Ornstein Email

Mike Ornstein's connection to the Saints dated back to 2006 when the Saints drafted Reggie Bush. As Bush's then marketing agent, Ornstein acquainted himself with the franchise and soon became an ally of Sean Payton.

In 2010, *The Times Picayune* explained Ornstein's relationship with the Saints thusly:[107]

> While not an official employee of the Saints, Ornstein has been a fixture at practices, games and in the locker room since the Saints drafted Bush in April 2006. He often wears team gear and is a regular presence on the sideline and on the field during practices.
>
> Payton devoted a chapter in his recent book about how valuable an asset Ornstein was to the team during its Super Bowl championship season. Ornstein was a point man for the Saints during their trip to Miami for the Super Bowl, arranging everything from daily gifts for players and their wives to strategically placed Saints billboards throughout the city. Ornstein also helps Payton with business arrangements outside of football, including the book deal and a movie script that Payton was working on last year.

By the time the Bountygate accusations surfaced Ornstein was a twice-convicted felon, most recently for scalping Super Bowl tickets and selling NFL jerseys fraudulently represented as game-worn.[108] Prior, in 1995, Ornstein plead guilty to mail fraud for attempting to defraud the NFL of $350,000 during his employment as an NFL marketing executive.[109]

Certainly, the NFL's opinion of Mike Ornstein was less than favorable.

Early in the Bountygate accusations, the NFL leaked a memo to *CBS'* Mike Freeman that allegedly detailed an email Mike Ornstein sent to Sean Payton pledging $5,000 for a bounty on Aaron Rodgers in a 2011 game.[110] The NFL corroborated this when they punished Sean Payton, noting "prior to the Saints' opening game in 2011, Coach Payton received an email from a close associate that stated in part, "PS Greg [sic] Williams put me down for $5000 on Rogers [sic]."[111]

Important or not, Aaron Rodgers finished the game in question uninjured even after being hit five times and sacked twice according to official NFL statistics.[112] If the Saints were intent on injuring Rodgers that night, they certainly had the opportunity yet didn't do so.

Regardless, Mike Ornstein would contest the NFL's characterization of this email, and eventually the *Associated Press* received a complete copy of the email's contents. First positioned by the NFL as sent from Ornstein to Payton for the purposes of pledging a bounty, the email was in fact sent to Greg Bensel (the Saints' SVP of Communications).

Bensel then forwarded the email to several Saints' coaches with a subject line that read: "Orny ... asked that I send it ... the dude is in prison so I told him I would."[113]

More important, the "bulk of the email" relayed Ornstein's experiences in prison. As a postscript Ornstein included the alleged bounty pledge on Rodgers, one that he insisted was part of a running joke. The *AP* described Ornstein's response to the bounty accusation like this:[114]

> "It's a running joke going for three years," Ornstein said in a phone interview this week, explaining that he had been kidding Williams about bounties ever since the NFC championship game in 2010, after which the Vikings told the NFL that they believed the Saints had a bounty on quarterback Brett Favre.

Mike Florio at *Pro Football Talk* reported that Ornstein said[115] "When I wrote that email, I was in jail. How was I going to pay for it? In stamps? I'm in federal jail in Florence."

Further, *ESPN's* Adam Schefter (along with NFL and NFLPA lawyers) obtained a text message from Gregg Williams to Mike Ornstein in which Williams reiterated Ornstein's response to the allegations. The text message from Williams read:[116]

> I stood up for you & told [the NFL] just that. I told them we never took that shut [sic] serious. I never ever saw you ever give $ and that's just the truth.

Again, it's a fair critique to contest the credibility of Mike Ornstein. But what's inarguable is the NFL's initial slanted characterization of the email versus its vetted reality. And as these realities emerged, they delineated a pattern that cast the NFL in a less-than-truthful light.

Expanding on this issue, Peter Ginsberg (Vilma's attorney) said in an interview with the *Associated Press*:[117]

> Ornstein's email is just another example of the speciousness of the quote-unquote evidence that Commissioner Goodell claims to have to support his erroneous accusations against Jonathan and the other players. As more of the evidence is revealed in the media, it is becoming more and more apparent how irresponsible the NFL's actions have been.

NFLPA counsel Richard Smith added:[118]

> The NFL has not provided the players with any information like this. It is unfortunate that they continue to withhold evidence that can show players' innocence. This email proves what we have feared: what they've been selling to the media as evidence doesn't match up with the truth.

6.) The Bounty Ledger

On June 1st, Jason Cole of *Yahoo!* broke a story that claimed the Saints kept a ledger of payments related to bounties on opponents. Specifically, Cole reported:[119]

> The NFL has a copy of a "ledger" that was kept detailing weekly earnings for players in the New Orleans Saints bounty system, according to two sources with knowledge of the investigation.
>
> The ledger, which shows both money earned for "cart-offs" and "whacks" and deducted for "mental errors," also points to the fact that players were told on a week-by-week basis of their performance ...
>
> Two specific entries for the 2009 season were shown ...

Perhaps most revealing, the NFL identified only two games (out of 54 played during the implicated timeframe) that supposedly detailed "bounties" on opponents.

Jason Cole originally reported those games were the Saints' 2009 game against the Buffalo Bills and the Saints' 2009 game against the New York Giants. Nothing from 2010. Nothing from 2011.

Soon after Cole reported this, Mike Florio of *Pro Football Talk* (in addition to a litany of Saints' fans across social media and message boards) roundly debunked the claims of injury in the Bills' game where

Saints' defenders, according to the NFL, were supposedly rewarded three separate $1,000 payments for "cart-offs."

In that game four Bills' players were injured, but three of those players were Bills' defenders. The other player was an offensive tackle. The accusation was nonsensical. It was impossible for Saints' defenders to have injured three players they didn't even play against.

Mike Florio reported these inconsistencies at 9:11 PM ET on June 1st, saying "there are several explanations. The most likely is that the ledger isn't accurate, and thus not entirely reliable."[120]

By 11:56 PM ET that same night, the NFL amended its report on the bounty ledger. They now claimed the three $1,000 bounty payments happened in a November 2009 game against the Carolina Panthers. That, though, turned out to be a specious claim as well. After all, only one player left that game with an injury: Panthers' LB Thomas Davis who, again, Saints' defenders couldn't have injured because they didn't play against him. In fact, Thomas incurred a non-contact injury while backpedaling into coverage during the fourth quarter.[121]

A popular Saints' blog, The Angry Who Dat blog, presented a complete analysis of the Panthers' game in an effort to understand the NFL's claims. If it was true, as the NFL claimed, that Saints' defenders received three different $1,000 bonuses for "cart-offs," then what plays generated those rewards?

About this, The Angry Who Dat blog surmised:[122]

> If the ledger is real, and if it details [three] 1,000-dollar payouts in the Carolina game, it's clear that they weren't for cart-offs or knockouts or whatever else you want to call them. [They] were "payable" big plays, but nothing as sinister as the league would have you believe. Again, we find ourselves having to stress the distinction between pay-for-performance bonuses, which are illegal, and pay-for-injury bounties, which are reprehensible if real.

Mike Florio corroborated the account from the Angry Who Dat blog, cited its work, and said:[123]

> Even then, the injuries that were inflicted in that game don't seem to match the notion that three Panthers were carted off.
>
> The end result is an even murkier mess that can never be clarified until raw evidence is released. Given the manner in

which the league's characterization of two items of evidence that have made their way to the media (i.e., the Anthony Hargrove declaration and the Mike Ornstein email) failed to correctly reflect their actual contents, there's no reason to believe that any description or summary of raw evidence from the league is or will be accurate.

How do we know what the ledger actually says until the ledger itself can be examined, objectively and independently? Given the glitches in Friday's reporting, and the lingering question regarding whether three Panthers players were in fact carted off or otherwise knocked out of the game with injury, it's entirely possible that the $1,000 payments were for big -- and legal -- hits that inflicted no harm of any kind.

This wasn't the end of this episode, though. In an October 9th memo to all NFL teams ("Report on Further Proceedings in Bounty Matter"), Roger Goodell once again amended the game in which these three $1,000 rewards supposedly occurred. This time, he claimed the Saints paid out the bonuses after a November 2010 game against the Carolina Panthers.[124]

First it was the Buffalo Bills' game in 2009. When skeptics proved that claim faulty, the NFL amended it to the Carolina Panthers' game in November 2009. When that didn't quite add up either, they changed it yet again to the Carolina Panthers' game in November 2010.

Indeed, Goodell reported in the aforementioned memo:[125]

> After a 2010 game against the Carolina Panthers ... three Carolina players were seriously injured: running backs Jonathan Stewart and Tyrell Sutton, who were literally carted off the field with a head/neck and ankle injury, respectively, and quarterback Matt Moore, who was later placed on injured reserve, unable to return for the remainder of the season, with a torn labrum.

These basic facts were true. The problem? None of the three players was injured on an illegal or sinister hit. The official play-by-play recap of this game confirmed that all three Panthers' players were injured on legal plays.[126] Furthermore, nowhere did the NFL establish that the Saints intentionally targeted -- i.e., placed a premeditated "bounty" -- on any of these players. These injuries occurred during the natural course of play as a result of accepted, legal football activity. This was a routine occurrence that happens on a weekly basis in all NFL games.

Lastly, the NFL also failed to establish a verifiable cash transaction -- that money indeed changed hands -- as a result of these legal, impactful plays. Yet according to Roger Goodell, this was evidence of a malicious, targeted injury program.

***

The other game in question on the supposed bounty ledger, the Saints-Giants 2009 game, also presented inconclusive evidence of bounties.

In that game, the NFL claimed Roman Harper received a $1,000 reward for injuring Giants' runningback Brandon Jacobs. *Sports Illustrated's* Peter King corroborated the NFL's claim via Twitter. King said:[127]

> NFL also showed evidence on ledger that S Roman Harper once was due $1000 for knocking NYG RB Brandon Jacobs from a game.

This, however, was another faulty claim. During the game in question, Brandon Jacobs only temporarily departed after a legal, unpenalized hit from Darren Sharper. The league's official play-by-play recap confirmed this.[128] Jacobs returned to the game and played.

If Roman Harper was indeed paid a $1,000 bonus after this game -- this was never established, only suggested -- then perhaps he earned a reward for a legal sack of Eli Manning that resulted in a fumble, that the Saints later converted into a touchdown right before the first half ended. Might this have been the source for the reward allegedly assigned to Harper?

Regardless, the shifting, unconvincing nature of the bounty ledger continued to erode the validity of the NFL's position. Not only were these "ledger" allegations not backed by evidence of premeditated targeting, they didn't result in illegal, malicious on-field activity, nor did they ever establish that any money actually changed hands. Instead, they identified plays that were routine, nondescript, legal events that happened during the accepted course of play.

Furthermore, the fact that this ledger identified only two of 54 games -- less than four percent of the Saints' games during the incriminated timeframe -- illustrated that the claims of paid, targeted bounties were far from reality.

7.) "Ducks in a Row"

As part of the NFL's intent to prove Sean Payton and Saints' coaches obstructed the league's investigation, the NFL attributed a phrase to Payton that indicated the Saints were covering up the existence of a bounty program.

Payton's alleged phrase, specifically, was "let's make sure our ducks are in a row."

In assessing penalties to the Saints' coaches and management, the NFL described Payton's alleged obfuscation this way:[129]

> In early 2010, Mr. Loomis advised Coach Payton that the league office was investigating allegations concerning a bounty program. Coach Payton said that he met with his top two defensive assistants, Coach Williams and Coach Vitt, in advance of the interview with league investigators and told them, "Let's make sure our ducks are in a row."
>
> Remarkably, Coach Payton claimed that he never inquired of Coach Williams and Coach Vitt as to what happened in the interviews, never asked them if a "pay-for-performance" or bounty program was in fact in place, and never gave any instructions to discontinue such a program.

By definition, this phrase wasn't inherently revealing of a conspiracy to hide the truth. At its root, it's a phrase that simply suggests the concept of organization. The phrase itself does not imply wrongdoing. Without knowing the full context of this phrase's usage, and without comment from Payton on his intent when employing this phrase, the words themselves were benign and revealing of little.

Unfortunately, the NFL didn't take the additional steps to ascertain the phrase's context and intent. Instead, they simply intimated that Payton's intent was mendacious when allegedly making that remark.

Payton might have simply been instructing his coaches to make sure they were fully prepared and organized for their meetings with NFL investigators; the phrase itself was never proof that Payton was in fact suggesting that his assistants lie, even though the NFL suggested that it was.

The NFL simply connected this phrase to the concept of a cover-up, and allowed perception to shape Payton's presumed guilt.

Not until Payton's reinstatement in early 2013 did Payton have the opportunity to address this comment. He told *Pro Football Talk's* Mike Florio:[130]

> I think more than anything else it just meant be prepared and, listen, I've read and seen a lot of the reports about what that was insinuating and I think, you know, we're stretching it or really looking for something there.
>
> It really wasn't what I was insinuating at all.

8.) The Alleged Favre Bounty and the Handwritten Note

The most well-publicized of the Bountygate allegations was the alleged bounty on Brett Favre in the NFC Championship game in January of 2010.

In Roger Goodell's statement on player punishments,[131] Goodell disciplined Jonathan Vilma for "[offering] a specific bounty -- $10,000 in cash -- to any player ... who knocked Minnesota quarterback Brett Favre out of the 2009 NFC Championship Game..."

This allegation immediately took on a life of its own, as Vilma and a host of Saints' players adamantly denied the claim. The source of this allegation was disgruntled, former Saints' coach Mike Cerullo (much more on him later) who provided to the NFL a transcribed note apparently detailing a bounty on Favre.

This note supposedly originated from a team meeting the night prior to the Saints-Vikings' NFC Championship Game when Vilma allegedly offered the bounty. When the NFL officially released its sixteen exhibits of evidence on June 15th (three days prior to the players' appeals), they included a transcription of this note as evidence. This, according to the NFL, was proof of the Favre bounty.

The first, obvious problem with this note was that it was a transcription, not the actual note itself. Apparently, the NFL transcribed it from Mike Cerullo's recollection from years earlier. The note itself referenced a "QB Out Pool" which the NFL claimed indicated a bounty.

The NFL's transcription revealed four individuals who supposedly pledged money to the "QB Out Pool": Jonathan Vilma, Charles Grant, Mike Ornstein, and Joe Vitt. The associated dollar amounts totaled

$35,000: $10,000 attributed to Vilma, $10,000 attributed to Grant, $10,000 attributed to Ornstein, and $5,000 attributed to Vitt.

The NFL's characterization of a $10,000 bounty (for months prior) suddenly morphed into a whopping $35,000. By June 18th, *ESPN* reported the change in a blog post from Kevin Seifert titled "NFL: Bounty on Brett Favre at least $35,000."[132]

This was yet another indication of an investigation lacking in reliable, consistent facts. Had the NFL believed the alleged bounty offer was $35,000 from the start, it was plausible to think they would have revealed that amount -- and not the $10,000 number. This might have been a peripheral issue (in that it didn't alter the NFL's ultimate accusation), but it was nevertheless another inconsistency in the NFL's claims.

As we learned with the other evidence, there were ample problems with this claim too -- both the note's transcription and the associated bounty accusations.

In a June 30th legal complaint, Peter Ginsberg said of the note:[133]

> The NFL did not produce the original document ... the document is not dated, the NFL did not identify the date of the creation of the original document, if such a document exists, or of the typed document.

This is obviously important because without a verified, dated original any person can allege any thing via transcribed evidence. It's only someone's unsubstantiated word put to paper.

This same brief from Ginsberg revealed that Charles Grant, who allegedly pledged $10,000, wasn't even present at the meeting where this bounty allegedly originated. The associated item from the legal complaint read:[134]

> One of the notations on the list is "QB Grant -- $10,000." Charles Grant was on injured reserve for the game in question. Upon information and belief, Grant did not attend the pre-game meeting before the 2009 NFC Championship game, to which Exhibit 10 supposedly relates.

If Grant wasn't even there, is it believable that he pledged a $10,000 bounty during the meeting? If no, doesn't that invalidate the reliability of the note itself?

Joe Vitt's inclusion in contributing $5,000 to the bounty was also a false accusation. Of the claim, Vitt said on June 20th:[135]

> I did not pledge any money for any incentive, pay for performance, bounty or any other alleged program in connection with any game, including the 2010 NFC Championship.
>
> Finally, it cannot be emphasized enough, none of our players, particularly those who are facing suspensions, ever crossed the white line with the intent to injure an opponent.

After Vitt's statement, the NFL exonerated Vitt of this accusation and confirmed he did not offer $5,000. Yet the NFL nevertheless submitted a piece of evidence that claimed Vitt did so. This disconnect, mostly, illuminated the unreliability of the note, and of Mike Cerullo.

NFL attorney Adolpho Birch asserted that the NFL couldn't corroborate the claims of Vitt pledging $5,000. Birch said this:[136]

> The short answer is no, we did not consider that as part of what formed the basis of [Vitt's] discipline. As we have stated before, what we did from an investigation standpoint is to look for things that were corroborated, and with respect to that particular point, there was no additional corroboration that would lead us to have the same level of confidence as many of the other things that we found.

Simply put, the NFL determined that the portion of the note detailing Vitt's role was unreliable. Because of that, they never formally disciplined Vitt for that potential transgression. At the same time, the NFL continued to tout the validity of the note as proof of a bounty on Favre.

How could one portion of the note be valid, while another part was deemed unreliable? How credible could Mike Cerullo's information be if he mistook or falsified basic events?

Further invalidating the legitimacy of the bounty on Favre was Mike Ornstein's denial of corroborating Vilma's $10,000 pledge. According to an official NFL transcript from June 18th, Mary Jo White, while representing the NFL, claimed:[137]

> Mr. [Gregg] Williams and Mr. [Mike] Ornstein and another member of the Saints defensive coaching staff, all of whom were

present at the meeting, all stated to NFL investigators that Mr. Vilma pledged $10,000 to any player who knocked Brett Favre out of the next week's NFC championship game against the Minnesota Vikings.

This testimony implicating Ornstein apparently supported the transcribed note. Ornstein, though, refuted White's assertion. In an interview with *Pro Football Talk's* Mike Florio on June 19th, Ornstein said:[138]

> I never corroborated $10,000. The only thing that I told them was that we had the [pregame] meeting, we jumped around, we screamed around, and I never saw [Vilma] offer one dime. And I never heard him say it.
>
> Did I say to the league that I saw Jonathan Vilma offer $10,000? Absolutely not.

Florio added this about his interview with Ornstein:[139]

> I asked Ornstein the question several different ways, to ensure there was no ambiguity. He consistently and repeatedly (and at times profanely) denied ever telling the NFL that Vilma offered money to anyone who knocked Favre and/or Warner out of the 2009 playoff games.

As was emblematic of the NFL's case by this point, these were additional examples of damning claims from the NFL -- those purporting to be evidence that supported their version of the truth -- that were later contested and proven unreliable or completely untrue.

What appeared to be happening was that the NFL was simply characterizing events and testimony in a manner that was favorable to their narrative, regardless of whether those characterizations were accurate or true.

In late July, Joe Vitt, Jonathan Vilma, and six Saints' teammates (current and former) testified under oath in federal court that Vilma -- nor anyone else -- placed a bounty on Brett Favre.

Those players were Roman Harper, Sedrick Ellis, Jonathan Casillas, Scott Shanle, Troy Evans, and Randall Gay. The NFL, on the other hand, presented no one to testify under oath, in court, that Vilma indeed pledged a bounty on Brett Favre.

Vilma explained to *ESPN's* Ed Werder:[140]

> Everybody was sworn in under oath in front of a judge with the risk of perjury and jail time if we were lying, and categorically denied there was a bounty. Seven people testified, 2 sworn affidavits all saying the same thing. I ask that you and ESPN report the facts.

Under the weight of scrutiny, the NFL's claim that Jonathan Vilma (and/or other Saints' employees) pledged a bounty on Brett Favre continued to crumble upon inspection.

By December when Paul Tagliabue voided all player discipline, the alleged bounty on Favre failed to hold up in its authenticity. Though Tagliabue stated that "I find there is more than enough evidence to support Commissioner Goodell's findings that Mr. Vilma offered such a bounty,"[141] Tagliabue then refused to issue *any* discipline to Vilma.

Had there been evidence of an actual bounty, it's reasonable to think Tagliabue would have upheld Goodell's ruling. Why if Tagliabue truly believed there was a large bounty on Brett Favre would he not have held Jonathan Vilma accountable for it?

Tagliabue may have believed there was evidence to "support" Goodell's findings, but he apparently didn't believe that the evidence *proved* anything. To the contrary.

Most revealing, Tagliabue stated this in his final ruling on Jonathan Vilma:[142]

> Adding to the complexity, there is little evidence of the tone of any talk about a bounty before the Vikings game. Was any bounty pledged serious? Was it inspirational only? Was it typical "trash talk" that occurs regularly before and during games? The parties presented no clear answers. No witness could confirm whether Vilma had any money in his hands as he spoke; no evidence was presented that $10,000 was available to him for purposes of paying a bounty or otherwise.
>
> There was no evidence that Vilma or anyone else paid any money to any player for any bounty-related hit on an opposing player in the Vikings game. I neither excuse nor condone the alleged offer of a bounty on Favre, whether offered by any player, coach, other Saints' employee or third party ...
>
> I cannot, however, uphold a multi-game suspension where there is no evidence that a player's speech prior to a game was

actually a factor causing misconduct on the playing field and that such misconduct was severe enough in itself to warrant a player suspension or a very substantial fine.

Tagliabue's actions spoke loudly. In referring to the Favre bounty, Tagliabue notably called it an "alleged offer of a bounty on Favre." After reviewing all of the information available, after presiding over the cross examination of a litany of parties, Tagliabue still called the bounty offer "alleged." He did this, presumably, because the offer was never proven to be true.

Tagliabue referenced "little evidence," "no clear answers," "no witness" to confirm allegations, "no evidence" that money was paid by or even available to Vilma, and no "misconduct on the playing field."

The proof was both in Tagliabue's deed and in his words.

***

With this body of evidence present by mid-June, the players were preparing for their first round of appeals with Roger Goodell. Months later in the Bountygate chronology, two more important pieces of evidence would surface -- signed declarations from Gregg Williams and Mike Cerullo -- and I'll cover those as we encounter them in our timeline.

But for the most part, the majority of the pre-cursor evidence used to ignite this boiling cauldron of stagecraft had made its way into the public arena by this time.

Equally significant the players' first legal challenges had failed in early June. Special Master Stephen Burbank rejected on procedural grounds the NFLPA's System Arbitration filing that challenged Roger Goodell's jurisdiction to rule on the bounty matter. Burbank ruled,[143] according to NFL spokesman Greg Aiello:

> System Arbitrator Stephen Burbank upheld the commissioner's authority under the collective bargaining agreement to impose 'conduct detrimental' discipline on players who provided or offered to provide financial incentives to injure opponents.

Burbank also importantly added in his ruling that he was making a determination only on the specifics of jurisdiction, and not making a judgment on the facts supporting the case. He said:[144]

It is important to emphasize -- with respect to all of the Players -- that nothing in this opinion is intended to convey a view about the underlying facts or the appropriateness of the discipline imposed.

The second legal filing, the Non Injury Grievance that challenged Goodell's right to discipline players for any conduct prior to the signing of the current collective bargaining agreement (August 4th, 2011), also failed. Arbitrator Shyam Das ruled that the CBA, in his view, did not prevent Roger Goodell from disciplining players for "conduct detrimental" prior to August 4th, 2011.

Das ruled:[145]

> It does not, as I read it, constitute an agreement by the NFL that the Commissioner relinquishes authority to impose discipline for conduct detrimental occurring prior to the execution of the CBA on August 4, 2011.

Though these first legal challenges by the NFLPA failed, the players were not out of options. Subsequent iterations of the appeals' process allowed for additional challenges, and those would continue.

In the meantime, with the first round of procedural challenges out of the way, the NFL prepared to hear the first of the players' appeals on June 18th.

Bountygate was in full throat.

12: "pure fantasy" -- or -- "what the hell are you doing, roger?"

Two weeks' prior to the players' first round of appeals on June 18th, Saints' linebacker Scott Shanle offered insight into the bounty accusations. More specifically, Shanle clarified the Saints' defense's incentive program to *The Times Picayune's* Mike Triplett.

Shanle explained that the Saints operated a pay-for-performance, not pay-to-injure, program that rewarded defenders for legal, impactful plays. This meant nominal bonuses for forced fumbles, interceptions, sacks, or any number of other plays that impacted the game in the Saints' favor. If Saints' defenders incidentally hurt an opponent in the course of making a legal play, they were also due a bonus -- not for specifically injuring their opponent, but for making an impactful, legal play.

Shanle was careful to explain that the Saints never explicitly set out to injure opponents, that their intent was not malicious or premeditated in any way. Equally important Shanle relayed that under this program, Saints' defenders were fined for penalties or illegal hits. Indeed, built into the Saints' pay-for-performance program was a disincentive for playing outside of the rules.

As Triplett noted, "Shanle did say firmly, 'I never saw any money for injuring somebody exchange hands'."[146]

More comprehensively, Triplett reported:[147]

> Shanle described ... a pay-for-performance program, which included payouts in the range of $500 and $1,000 for a variety of big plays, including big hits...
>
> But Shanle said that didn't mean the intent or purpose of the pay-for-performance system was to target players for injuries...
>
> Shanle said those terms ("cart-off," "knockout," "kill the head") were used "in Gregg's language" ... whose over-the-top motivational tactics have been well-documented. But Shanle insisted that players didn't take Williams literally...

[Shanle] said players would lose money just as easily as gaining money, thanks to fines for penalties and mental errors. So penalties or illegal hits were actually discouraged.

At this point, this was the clearest indication of the alleged "system" in place on the Saints' defense. It sharply differed from Roger Goodell's portrayal of a targeted injury system that routinely singled-out opponents for injury, and then rewarded Saints' defenders for the infliction of an injury.

The difference in these two systems was vast, and Goodell's attempt to blur the lines between the two indicated that he wasn't interested in relaying factual content.

Instead, he was more interested in distorting events in order to send a variety of messages -- that the NFL cared for player safety, that they were actively policing supposed malicious activity, that they would sternly discipline anyone who strayed beyond the bounds of legality, and that the NFL's violent nature wasn't systemic to the league's culture but rather a result of a few isolated, rogue individuals.

That Goodell's claims were largely faulty was apparently of secondary importance; at this point in the NFL's history, relaying these messages trumped reality, facts, due process, precedence, and fairness.

When the NFL submitted their sixteen official exhibits of evidence on June 15th, the evidence totaled 200 pages. In March, the NFL claimed it had reviewed 50,000 pages of documentation. When it came time to show their cards, when they were legally forced to do so, the NFL produced a microscopic .4% of that supposed 50,000 page total as evidence.

Moreover, of the 200 pages submitted, 31 of those pages (15.5%) did not even exist when the NFL officially levied the Bountygate allegations. They didn't exist when the NFL punished the coaches in late March. And they didn't exist when the NFL punished the players in early May.

Specifically, those pages contained a rambling, incomprehensible 10,000-word manifesto from Sean Pamphilon[148] (written on May 31st, 2012) and the previously mentioned Mike Triplett article (dated June 5th, 2012).

Laughably, the NFL included these materials as official evidence -- even though the NFL didn't produce them as a result of their investigation, and even though they weren't in existence when the NFL punished all of the accused parties. Lastly those pages were suggestive of nothing incriminating, of nothing that proved targeted, rewarded injuring of opponents.

This absurdity was emblematic of the NFL's investigation, its characterizations, and its official evidence.

The majority of the submitted material contained information completely unrelated to any program operated by the Saints' defense. Many of the exhibits included motivational urgings ("the inner voice"); checklists of attendance during practices and training sessions; preparatory notes for the players' weekly schedule; diet, hydration, and hygiene reminders; game-specific strategy assignments, positional alignments, opponent tendencies ("the first 15"), etc.; and presentation slides lampooning former Saints Mike Karney, Marc Bulger, and Jake Delhomme.

There were slides detailing "game fees" and "game dues," but there was little context beyond names, numbers, and vague terminology.

Some of this material tallied tackle counts, big plays, and yards-after-the-catch-surrendered by Saints' defenders. The previously-mentioned terminology included "MOBP – missed opportunity for a big play," "ME – mental error," "loaf," "cart-off," "kill the head," "whack," and "impact play."

Nowhere did these terms explicitly define or suggest targeted injuries and associated rewards.

The larger problem was that the NFL failed to clarify the meaning of these terms. If the NFL refused to learn their actual meaning and context, it would perhaps allow them to infuse those terms with a sinister spin that wasn't factually accurate. It appeared to be a strategy of willful ignorance.

In their June 18th "Annotated Version of Exhibits," the NFLPA revealed:[149]

> Despite the length of the Commissioner's investigation and the experience of those involved, the fact is that the slides provided by the NFL, and relied upon as a basis for discipline, were never shown to any Saints coaches for explanation by NFL Investigators.

As a result of the NFL's failure to ascertain the meaning of these terms, the NFLPA conducted its own investigation to define their meaning. Under the leadership of Executive Director DeMaurice ("De") Smith, the NFLPA interviewed "relevant personnel [including current and former Saints players, coaches, and individuals who attended all defensive meetings]."

In relation to the terminology's true meaning, this is what the NFLPA discovered:[150]

"Cart-off"

> A "cart-off" is simply a hard hit. It does not literally mean that a player was carted off the field. Coaches and players may use the terms "Knockout," "Tapout," "Blowups," or "Hit Parade" to describe the same type of play.

"Whack"

> The best way for a small tackler to take on a larger player; it is more commonly called a "Crossbody Tackle." Saints players were often times undersized and Coach Williams used this term to try to improve tackling technique.

"Kill the Head"

> Part of Coach Williams' "defend every blade of grass" strategy ... Its strategy was to get RB's and WR's to mentally vacate the game. The logic is that if you allowed RB's and WR's to run straight at you and successfully penetrate your defense, then you would basically validate their superiority. You would by default present a passive approach to defense. The result of this would be catastrophic to any defensive game plan.

"Impact play"

> A 4th quarter play when the game was on the line. Usually with less than 2 possessions left. It could be any number of plays, whether it be a great tackle, interception or a pass breakup. It could be a team effort like a strategic stop that denies the offense yardage or touchdowns.

"ME"

> Refers to "mental errors," failing to perform as coached or diverting from the game plan. For example, losing focus and

behaving in an automatic manner that is contrary to what the team scheme is.

"Loaf"

When Coach Williams arrived in New Orleans, he wanted to make clear exactly what he wanted in the form of effort. So this was a way [for] Coach Williams to teach and measure effort.

"MOBP"

A Missed Opportunity for Big Play. For example, a pass breakup but missed interception, or a sack but a missed strip. It's an opportunity loss.

Nowhere did this information indicate an intent to injure, or to reward injuries inflicted. This terminology much more closely correlated with Shanle's description of a pay-for-performance program than it did with the NFL's characterization of a bounty program.

***

Also included in the NFL's official evidence was the transcription of the "note" that allegedly indicated the Favre bounty. Under scrutiny, as we just saw, this note proved contradictory and unreliable, including portions of which were provably false.

In addition, several Saints' employees testified under oath in federal court as to the note's misrepresentation of the truth in denying the Favre bounty ever existed.

These 200 pages of official evidence also contained a second email from Mike Ornstein; the first email (addressed in the previous chapter) was not included with the official exhibits of evidence. Ornstein sent this second email, dated October 12th, 2009, directly to Gregg Williams.

It read, in full:[151]

Dickhead I gave you 1500 last week, I will give you another 1500 for the next 4 game, and the final 2000 for the last 4.

Without providing any further context beyond this one sentence, the NFL apparently included this email as a suggestion of a bounty pledge from Ornstein.

But according to Ornstein, as revealed in legal documents submitted by Peter Ginsberg, this email related to Ornstein's financial contributions to Gregg Williams' charity.

In the legal brief "Jonathan Vilma Versus The National Football League," Peter Ginsberg explained:[152]

> Ornstein communicated directly to Goodell that the email, in fact, concerned Ornstein's contributions to a charitable organization run by Williams, that he had contributed NFL merchandise rather than money to the organization for years, that he no longer had access to NFL merchandise, and he instead was contributing money for the Williams charitable organization.
>
> Ornstein further requested Goodell to corroborate his explanation of the email by obtaining financial documents of Williams' charitable organization that reflected donations.
>
> Upon information and belief, the NFL never sought to obtain financial documents relating to Williams' charitable organization.

Whether one finds Ornstein's claim believable, the intimation by the NFL that this email suggested a bounty pledge was flimsy nonetheless. Nowhere did that email connect to an explicit pledge of rewarding any player for any deed, malicious or otherwise. It was not proof of anything, only suggestive of what any person might imagine it suggested.

More important, once again, the NFL submitted a piece of evidence that the accused parties ultimately proved flawed. Like the NFL's failure to learn the meaning behind the aforementioned terminology, this failure to understand the context of Ornstein's email once again indicated that the NFL wasn't concerned with uncovering the full truth. Instead, they were apparently inclined to offering anecdotal evidence that would, only on its surface, support their accusations.

Like many of their other claims, the credibility of this claim collapsed upon inspection.

The lone piece of official evidence that was potentially incriminating was this strange slide:[153]

- Background study on suspects?
- Size, WT., Picture?
- Toughness, Strength, Fighting Skills?
- Armed and dangerous?
- Mental State of Suspect? Deranged???
- Escape routes covered to prevent escape?
- Must suspect be delivered dead or alive?
- All things researched, prepared, & ready to go?
- Now its time to do our job...collect bounty$$$!
- No apologies! Let's go Hunting!

Regrettably Dog the Bounty Hunter (of recent pop culture notoriety) appeared next to a phrase stating "collect bounty$$$!" and "[l]et's go hunting!" Whether this was meant as a literal exhortation was up for debate, especially considering some of the other information on the slide.

When one considered obtuse phrases like "Armed and Dangerous?", "Mental State of Suspect? Deranged???", and "Must suspect be delivered dead or alive?", it was reasonable to conclude that this slide -- apparently used for motivational purposes -- was defined by hyperbole and not literal instructions.

Bolstering this interpretation, Scott Shanle told Mike Triplett[154] about Gregg Williams on June 5th: "Gregg said crazy stuff. If you take him literally, you're gonna be locked up."

***

Also important was the "evidence" the NFL did not include in their official set of exhibits: the Anthony Hargrove declaration and the bounty ledger, for two. Apparently due to the glaring flaws included in both of these allegations -- once presented as evidence of guilt -- the NFL decided against even including either of these as official evidence.

Further absent from the official evidence was any mention of a bounty on Kurt Warner, which the NFL punished Jonathan Vilma for allegedly offering. When forced to back up that claim and the resulting punishment, the NFL failed to produce anything that supported their accusation and discipline.

Most tellingly, the NFL also decided against producing any witnesses during the appeals' hearing to corroborate their claims against the players. Of that important development, Peter Ginsberg said[155] "that's because there are no credible witnesses who could substantiate the commissioner's allegations."

In the minutes prior to attending their appeals with Roger Goodell, the players (Fujita, Hargrove, and Smith) released a collective statement. It read:[156]

> We have purportedly been disciplined by the Commissioner for alleged activities that the National Football League has grossly misrepresented to the public. We are in attendance today not because we recognize the Commissioner's jurisdiction to adjudicate regarding these specious allegations, but because we believe the League would attempt to publicly mischaracterize our refusal to attend. We will not address the substance of the NFL's case because this is not the proper venue for adjudication, and there has been no semblance of due process afforded to us.
>
> As veteran players of 11, 9 and 9 years in this League, we are profoundly disappointed with the NFL's conduct in this matter. We know what the NFL has publicly said we did, and the Commissioner has chosen to try to punish us and disparage our characters based on semantics, not facts. Words are cheap and power is fleeting.
>
> Shame on the National Football League and Commissioner Goodell for being more concerned about '"convicting" us publicly than being honorable and fair to men who have dedicated their professional lives to playing this game with honor.

After the appeals' hearings ended on June 18th, Peter Ginsberg referred to the hearing as a "sham."[157] Vilma railed against Roger Goodell, accusing Goodell of destroying his professional reputation saying Goodell "[tore] down what I built over eight years."[158] Vilma continued: "I don't know how I can get a fair process when he is the judge, jury and executioner. You're assuming it will be fair, but it's not."[159]

Piling on, Scott Fujita said:[160] "The NFL's investigation has been highlighted by sensationalized headlines and unsubstantiated leaks to the media ... The NFL has been careless and irresponsible, and at some time will have to provide answers."

Ginsberg summed up the appeals' hearing like this:[161]

> Unfortunately, what it says to me is Commissioner Goodell has made a dreadful mistake. After what Jonathan and the other players have been put through, to suggest the players are being presented with any kind of fair hearing based on what has been presented today is pure fantasy.
>
> The thin production today doesn't link any of the players to a bounty system, and that's consistent with what we know to be true -- there was no bounty system.

In an apparent effort to quickly respond to these widespread protestations, the NFL hosted a private meeting soon after the appeals' hearing ended. For this meeting, the NFL summoned twelve members of the media and reviewed the evidence with them. This appeared to be a tactic aimed at convincing these individuals of the evidence's incriminating nature, and better controlling the message in the public domain.

Not included with the twelve attendees -- perhaps for being Bountygate's most vocal critic in the media -- Mike Florio called this an "Apostle-sized collection of scribes."[162] Moreover, what this event revealed was the NFL's fear of allowing the evidence and events to speak for themselves.

Instead of simply supplying the evidence in full to the players and their union, instead of allowing the public to judge the legitimacy of the source evidence, the NFL resorted to a secret meeting in which they attempted to shape the message to the media.

Such opacity was, at this point, a defining characteristic of Bountygate and this was yet another example.

***

On the night of the appeals, the NFLPA released a comprehensive, sixteen-point statement that condemned Roger Goodell's and the NFL's actions. The NFLPA stated[163] that Roger Goodell's investigation and subsequent process violated Goodell's "duty to refrain from resorting to improper methods to defend an unsubstantiated pronouncement." The NFLPA, in essence, directly accused Goodell of operating a fraudulent investigation and appeals' process.

Notably, the statement mentioned that the NFL failed to question any of the Saints' coaches about the evidence used as a basis for punishment; withheld evidence, then punished the players without allowing them to review or challenge the material; and drew false conclusions based on purposefully mischaracterized testimony.

Of the NFL and the media, the NFLPA rebuked the league[164] for "[launching] a public campaign in the media to support the discipline and tarnish the reputations of players before any hearing, effectively destroying any claim that the Commissioner could act as an impartial arbitrator."

In summary, NFLPA attorney Richard Smith stated:[165]

> In this matter, the conduct of the Commissioner and his representatives has undermined the fundamental process contemplated by the Collective Bargaining Agreement. Through this abuse, these players have been denied any semblance of due process and fairness.
>
> At a time when some question the safety and integrity of the game, the failure by those charged to act responsibly and fairly have challenged our collective faith and confidence in the league.

Echoing this sentiment on June 22nd, Scott Fujita appeared on Dave Zirin's *Edge of Sports* radio show on Sirius XM and relayed his opinions on Bountygate and the appeals' process.

When asked by Zirin if he did what the NFL accused him of doing, Fujita said "No. Absolutely not."[166]

Responding to Zirin's question about the NFL's claims of a pay-to-injure system, Fujita said:[167]

> I was there for one year in 2009, and, without question, there was nobody paying or receiving any money for causing injury. I've talked to enough guys who I'm close with who were there for the seasons after I left, and it's the same thing.
>
> The problem is that the league has billed this thing as being this super-organized pay-to-injure scheme, which it never was.

Fujita called his alleged involvement in Bountygate "a public smear campaign."[168]

Of his interactions with Roger Goodell in the aftermath of the accusations, Fujita said:[169]

> I saw him in the [appeal] hearings and he offered to shake all of our hands.
>
> Some of the other players didn't, but I went ahead and shook his hand, and I just said to him, "What the hell are you doing, Roger?"
>
> He had nothing to say. His face sure turned red, though.

***

With the players' first round of appeals completed, and with the hostility between the NFL and the accused players at a fevered pitch, Jonathan Vilma would soon file another lawsuit.

In it, Vilma would officially expose Bountygate's notorious, principal accuser: disgruntled ex-Saints' coach, Mike Cerullo.

13: mike cerullo, the disgruntled whistleblower

In early July, approximately two weeks after the players' first appeals, Jonathan Vilma sued the NFL in an attempt to have his suspension overturned, among other things. With the players still awaiting a ruling on their appeals, Vilma engaged in litigation as a second attack on the league's internal disciplining and sanctioning process which he believed deprived him of his legal rights under the NFL's collective bargaining agreement.

Vilma contested Roger Goodell's role as an impartial arbitrator (impartiality is a stipulation of the CBA); and Vilma further sought an injunction that would temporarily put his suspension on-hold while the case was adjudicated.

This was the second lawsuit filed by Vilma related to Bountygate. Vilma's first lawsuit targeted Roger Goodell specifically for defaming Vilma's character by making known false public statements. With this new lawsuit, Vilma was now battling separately both Roger Goodell and the NFL.

The NFLPA, concurrently, filed a similar suit on behalf on Scott Fujita, Anthony Hargrove, and Will Smith. Because Vilma secured legal representation outside of the NFLPA, he filed his own suit. But for the sake of the proceedings, these suits filed by Vilma and the NFLPA were essentially the same: they sought to overturn the suspensions.

Among the many submissions in Vilma's lawsuit, Peter Ginsberg summarized Vilma's contentions like this:[170]

> No system of American justice permits a person to be punished without having had the opportunity to substantively review, investigate and question the evidence and the sources of such evidence presented against him or her.
>
> The NFL violated these basic tenets of American jurisprudence by refusing to produce any evidence in a timely fashion, by refusing to produce the evidence requested by Vilma, by failing to disclose the purported sources of any of its purported evidence, and by failing to present the purported sources for cross-examination at the Appeal Hearing.

The NFL violated these basic tenets of American jurisprudence by allowing a person who previously had publicly pre-judged the merits of the allegations then serve as the arbitrator deciding the matter.

With both Goodell and the NFL squarely in the crosshairs of Vilma's lawsuits, this legal brief relayed several other key pieces of information in the then four month-long proceedings.

Vilma alleged that Roger Goodell had "issued a 'gag order' on Gregg Williams, prohibiting him from speaking with anyone about the Bounty Program investigation."[171]

In the same vein the suit stated that because Goodell would solely decide (at some point in the future) Gregg Williams' and Sean Payton's reinstatements, "Goodell effectively prohibited Williams and Payton from communicating with anyone but Goodell-approved people regarding the alleged Bounty Program and the manner and means by which the NFL conducted its investigation."[172]

By attempting to silence Payton and Williams, Goodell again revealed his refusal to conduct an open process. Goodell likely sought to prevent interested parties -- the accused, their attorneys, the media, etc. -- from developing a fuller, truer picture of the accusations by speaking with Payton or Williams. With this action theoretically providing fewer refutations for him to contest, Goodell retained a greater degree of control over the outcome of Bountygate.

Another note of significance from this legal brief reiterated the fact that the accused players rarely strayed from the rules of on-field play. Note #138 read:[173]

> The four players whom Goodell alleges were the leaders and participants of the Bounty Program combined received a total of nine penalties resulting in fines during the three years in which Goodell claims the Bounty Program existed.
>
> Vilma only received two fines during those three years, one for roughing the passer in 2009 and once for grabbing a facemask in 2010.

For individuals portrayed as malicious, rule-breaking miscreants, these four players rarely deviated from the accepted standards of play. In the Goodell-era NFL where the league aggressively fines players for on-field transgressions, the four accused players so infrequently invited the NFL's discipline that each player averaged less than one fineable offense per year.

Nine fine-worthy penalties in three seasons among the four players equated to 3/4th of *one* fine per season per player.

In a season where a player may participate in 800 plays, that would translate into each accused player engaging in fineable conduct a microscopic .094% percent of the time: not even one tenth of one percent.

For players who were allegedly the ringleaders of a three-year injury program, this made little sense. The data didn't support the NFL's portrayal.

This was again a reminder of why the NFL failed to discipline any player connected to Bountygate for any on-field misconduct: there was none to punish.

***

Included with the new information from this legal filing, the most notable revelation was Vilma's official outing of former Saints' defensive coach Mike Cerullo as the NFL's primary whistleblower. The associated legal brief outlined a series of points explaining Cerullo's role in Bountygate.

Pro Football Talk's Mike Florio explained:[174]

> The latest Jonathan Vilma lawsuit blows the whistle on many things regarding the bounty investigation. It also blows the whistle on the notorious whistleblower.
>
> Though it's been widely rumored that former Saints defensive assistant Mike Cerullo is the person who resurrected the bounty probe by reaching out to the league office in 2011, Vilma's civil complaint makes it clear that Vilma believes Cerullo created the present mess.
>
> Vilma also believes that Cerullo is acting out of spite.

Cerullo first surfaced as the potential whistleblower as far back as April 2012 but the confirmation of his identity remained speculation until Vilma filed this lawsuit. New Orleans' filmmaker Allen Donnes, who also authored a book on the Saints in 2007, first suggested Cerullo as the league's source during a radio interview on April 10th.

Donnes said:[175]

> Based on my sources, and I believe they're very good, the former defensive quality control coach, his name is Mike Cerullo with a 'C,' was let go after the Super Bowl season and for whatever reason, he was unable to find work in the NFL and he believed that it was Gregg Williams and Sean Payton and others in the Saints organization blocking him from getting other work. To the best of the sources I have and everybody else has, we all have that name.

Cerullo had come to the Saints' organization in 2007 by way of the Atlanta Falcons. Prior to that he had worked as an assistant with the Syracuse University football program, among other places.

By April of 2010 the Saints had fired Cerullo and for this, according to Vilma's second lawsuit, Cerullo "pledged revenge against the Saints, and particularly against Vitt, following his termination."[176]

Vilma's lawsuit further explained:[177]

> The Saints terminated Cerullo following various incidents, including disappearing from the Club during the 2009 Season and providing a pretextual excuse that was shown to be inaccurate and, again, disappearing from the Club during the week leading up to the Super Bowl in 2010, again giving a pretextual excuse that was shown to be inaccurate.

When testimony from Joe Vitt found its way into the public domain by January of 2013, the public learned more details about Cerullo's unexplained absences from the team and his apparent mendacious nature.

Of an early encounter with Mike Cerullo, Vitt explained:[178]

> Mike Cerullo, because I'm the assistant head coach, comes to me and tells me he's got financial problems, that his father has got cancer, that he's spending a lot of money back home for his father's chemotherapy. I fix him up with Dennis Lauscha. Dennis Lauscha is our president and CEO. Dennis helps him file for bankruptcy. I think we give him a little bit of money.
>
> Well, the first trip that we take as a staff out to Las Vegas to see some Las Vegas shows with our wives, here comes Mike Cerullo, pulls up with two limos, and two girls get out of each limo. So he's

just declared bankruptcy, but he can go buy - get two limos with a bunch of girls coming out ... the red light went off for me.

Of Cerullo's frequent absences from the team, which ultimately resulted in Cerullo's firing, Vitt relayed that Cerullo missed three weeks of the team's 16-week 2009 regular season schedule. Vitt explained each absence.[179] Vitt said this about Cerullo's first absence:

> The first time, he told us he had to go out and visit his fiancé and their kids, because there was a sickness in the family, his fiancé is an orthopedic surgeon, he had to help the kids get to school, there's some illness.

The second absence:

> Midseason he comes back and tells us ... [his] fiancé's brother has flown to Haiti to help with the Haiti Relief Fund after the earthquake. There's an aftershock, and her brother is now killed in the aftershock.

> She's got to get over there to identify the body, [Cerullo's] got to fly to Oklahoma to watch the kids. He's gone for another week.

The third absence:

> [Cerullo] comes to our team security guy, and he's got to go out there another week to retrieve an engagement ring that he gave to a girl ... So that's a third week.

That wasn't all, though. The week after the Saints' Super Bowl victory in 2010, Cerullo made another claim, presumably seeking more time away from the team. Vitt explained this scenario:

> A week after the season ends, it's a Friday night, I'm saying not more than a week after the Super Bowl. Sean Payton calls me on a Friday night. ... He said Mike Cerullo's fiancé was just in a terrible car accident down in Oklahoma. The truck overturned, a child was thrown from the car and was drowned in a pond.

By now skeptical of Cerullo's claims, Vitt offered to accompany Cerullo to Oklahoma by way of Tom Benson's private jet that same night. Cerullo refused the offer and declined any assistance from the team. This claim, like the others, Vitt and Payton believed to be a lie.

For what Peter Ginsberg referred to as Cerullo's "incompetence and repeated and material lies,"[180] the Saints fired Cerullo in April of 2010.

Then, following Cerullo's termination, the Saints were fearful enough of Cerullo's alleged vow for revenge that they hired police protection for Sean Payton.

Ginsberg explained:[181]

> The Saints were so concerned about Cerullo's stability, as Goodell also knew, that, when Cerullo was terminated, Saints head coach Sean Payton also was forced to obtain police protection at his house for fear that Cerullo would seek some type of retribution.

Irrespective of the multiplicity of damning circumstances that defined Cerullo's tenure in New Orleans -- incompetence, mendacity, apparent threats of revenge -- the NFL upheld Cerullo as the principal, credible source in the Bountygate accusations.

This early July lawsuit from Vilma stated "the NFL relied principally upon Cerullo's statements during its investigation into the alleged Bounty Program" and that the NFL "based its disciplinary decisions largely on Cerullo's statements."[182]

Even though the NFL touted "multiple, independent sources" in its investigation, the reality was that Cerullo -- a disgruntled ex-employee with a proven history of "material lies" who vowed revenge on the Saints -- almost single-handedly laid the groundwork for the bounty accusations.

Vitt further explained that the NFL publicly distorted their sourcing claims when Cerullo was in fact the league's sole source:[183]

> So this whole investigation has centered around Cerullo. It hasn't been what the investigators told me ... "[they] have it all corroborated."
>
> This whole thing is because of Mike Cerullo. Our general manager is suspended, the head coach is out for a full year because of Mike Cerullo? Mike Cerullo?
>
> Well, I told the investigators from Day 1 that's all they had? [They] got Mike Cerullo, and [they] got Gregg Williams? Two disgruntled employees that were fired? Gregg Williams was fired. Gregg Williams was fired. He had to crawl on his stomach to keep his job with the New Orleans Saints. When do we want to talk about Mike Cerullo? Do we want to talk about Cerullo yet?

> Mike Cerullo can tell you anything he wants ... let's cut to the chase. Mike Cerullo is a liar. Mike Cerullo is wrong.

Not only was Vitt's opinion of Mike Cerullo incontrovertibly damning, Vilma's suit alleged that Cerullo, at one point, retracted his claims in an April 2012 meeting with Roger Goodell:[184]

> According to a close associate of Cerullo's, who discussed the Bounty Program investigation with Cerullo on multiple occasions, Cerullo retracted his previous claims about the Bounty Program, including in a communication directly with Goodell that occurred in April 2012.

While this claim was never corroborated, it added further doubt as to Cerullo's veracity and credibility.

Regardless, Vilma's suit reported that the NFL never shared its notes of interviews with Cerullo, nor did they compel him to testify at the players' appeals.[185]

What this meant was that the disgruntled Cerullo made a variety of claims to the NFL; the NFL then characterized those claims in a manner they so chose; refused to support those claims with the source transcripts of their interviews with Cerullo; and then finally prevented Cerullo from testifying at the players' appeals where his credibility and claims could've been dismantled.

It was a process devoid of legitimacy and dripping with farce.

Lastly, and perhaps most important, Vilma's suit revealed:[186]

> Upon information and belief, Cerullo created Exhibit 10 (the handwritten note alleging the Favre bounty) well after the 2009 NFC Championship Game and in an effort to gain revenge against the Saints for terminating his employment.

***

This wouldn't be the last the public learned about Cerullo, his motives, and his lack of credibility. But that wouldn't happen until October when his declaration became public.

In the meantime, two days after Jonathan Vilma's July 1st lawsuit, Roger Goodell ruled on the players' appeals and upheld his original sanctions. Goodell ruled:[187]

> Throughout this entire process, including your appeals, and despite repeated invitations and encouragement to do so, none of you has offered any evidence that would warrant reconsideration of your suspensions ... Instead, you elected not to participate meaningfully in the appeal process ...

Imagine that: Roger Goodell accusing the players of not sharing evidence.

On cue, the NFL Players' Association soon released a response to Goodell's ruling. It read:[188]

> The players are disappointed with the League's conduct during this process. We reiterate our concerns about the lack of fair due process, lack of integrity of the investigation and lack of the jurisdictional authority to impose discipline under the collective bargaining agreement. Moreover, the Commissioner took actions during this process that rendered it impossible for him to be an impartial arbitrator.
>
> The NFLPA has never and will never condone dangerous or reckless conduct in football and to date, nothing the League has provided proves these players were participants in a pay-to-injure program. We will continue to pursue all options.

With that said, the appeals' process wasn't nearly finished. It would continue on to federal court, to an appeals' panel, to another disciplinary phase, and finally to Paul Tagliabue in the coming months.

While the appeals' process played out, the 2012 preseason was nearing. And with it, there was some good news for Saints' fans.

14: an investigation and an induction

In early June, the month before Roger Goodell issued his ruling on the players' appeals, Saints' owner Tom Benson hired Louis Freeh to conduct a comprehensive investigation into the Saints' organization.

This seemed like a significant development, as it would potentially address the lack of verifiable facts arising in the months after Bountygate surfaced.

Louis Freeh is a former FBI Director, federal judge, and federal attorney renowned for his role in several high-profile prosecutions during his time as a United States attorney. After his tenure as a federal attorney and judge, Freeh then served as the Director of the FBI from September 1993 through 2001.[189]

When his FBI duties concluded, Freeh worked in corporate law before ultimately founding *Freeh Group International Solutions* (*FGIS*) in 2007. Best described as an investigative and consulting firm, *FGIS* is an "independent global risk management firm serving in the areas of business integrity and compliance, safety and security, and investigations and due diligence."[190]

Just prior to being enlisted by Tom Benson, Louis Freeh led an investigation at Penn State after the much-publicized Jerry Sandusky pedophilia scandal. In that investigation, Freeh uncovered many of the underlying facts of the Sandusky-Penn State debacle in what was widely hailed as a "damning report."[191]

With Freeh's wide-ranging expertise and track record for integrity, Benson hired Freeh.

On Freeh's role in investigating the Saints, Saints' team spokesman Greg Bensel said:[192]

> Serious allegations have been made about our organization this off-season; we take these allegations very seriously.
>
> As a result, we have hired the Freeh Group, founded by former director of the FBI and former federal judge Louis Freeh. Mr. Benson moved quickly to hire them and has spared no expense to get to the bottom of these allegations. We have given the

Freeh Group complete access to our team and all of the individuals who have been associated with this news story.

Mike Florio opined on Freeh's role in New Orleans. He said:[193]

> From all indications, Freeh conducted a thorough investigation that pulled no punches and did no favors to anyone at Penn State. He and his investigative team appeared interested only in getting to the truth of what happened ...
>
> Given that, it's fair to conclude that if there's dirt to be found with the Saints, Freeh will find it.

By all appearances, this was a move by Tom Benson aimed at better understanding the dynamics of his organization; ascertaining facts from the many allegations lobbed; and perhaps making necessary organizational changes to ensure the team's long-term health.

What was not certain, though, was if Tom Benson would make public the findings of Freeh's investigation. Because the Saints are a private organization, Tom Benson was under no obligation to release the report's results or even announce the investigation's conclusion.

Whether Freeh completed his investigation, or is still conducting it, remains unknown. What's known is that the Saints made no structural changes to key positions in the months following Freeh's hiring. In fact, Saints' General Manager Mickey Loomis received a contract extension in August of 2012.[194]

This development might have been indicative of Freeh's findings: one could infer that if Mickey Loomis was indeed illegally eavesdropping or covering up a pay-to-injure program, then Tom Benson would be less inclined to reward Loomis with a new contract. But because Benson in fact rewarded Loomis with a contract extension in August, it lent credence to the inference that Freeh's discoveries were not damning.

Also in August of 2012, Tom Benson met privately with Roger Goodell in New York. Aside from the Saints and league sources confirming this meeting, there was no other news made available as to the substance of the talks. In early August, however, *ESPN* reported:[195]

> Saints owner Tom Benson has privately expressed his displeasure with Goodell on the severity of the sanctions that hit the franchise, including a year-long suspension of head coach

Sean Payton and an eight-game suspension of general manager Mickey Loomis, according to sources.

A week after *ESPN* reported this, Benson flew to New York for the aforementioned meeting with Goodell. Perhaps the results from Freeh's investigation revealed facts that did not align with the NFL's allegations. As a result, potentially, Benson decided to fly to New York to discuss the matter privately with Roger Goodell.

The logical inferences from Freeh's involvement in the months following his hiring did not paint a damning picture for the Saints: a contract extension for one of the accused principals of Bountygate; a report that Tom Benson was displeased with Goodell; and a Benson-initiated meeting with Roger Goodell thereafter. The timing of these events was, perhaps, indicative of facts uncovered by Freeh.

At any rate, Freeh's involvement was a positive development for both Bountygate and the Saints regardless of what it might reveal. It would potentially unearth facts instead of distortions, and it would help ensure the overall viability of the Saints' franchise.

For frustrated Saints' fans unsure of what was true and what wasn't, Freeh's involvement served to at least potentially get to the root of the matter. That alone was encouraging.

***

More encouraging for the Saints in the summer of 2012 was Willie Roaf's enshrinement in the Pro Football Hall of Fame. With Rickey Jackson enshrined in 2010, Roaf was the second former Saints' player elected to the Hall of Fame.

Willie Roaf was a product of Louisiana Tech, his father a dentist and his mother the first African-American woman to serve on the Arkansas Supreme Court. In 1993, the Saints selected Roaf with their first round draft pick (8th overall). Almost immediately, Roaf established himself as one of the best tackles in football.

From 1993 - 2001, Roaf manned the left tackle position in New Orleans and was named to the NFL's all-decade team of the 1990's. In 1994, '95, and '96, Roaf earned first-team All Pro honors; in 1997 and 2000, he was a second-team All-Pro.

In 2002, the Saints (regrettably) traded Roaf to the Kansas City Chiefs. There, Roaf played four seasons before retiring after the 2005 season. In three of his four seasons in Kansas City, Roaf garnered first-team All-Pro accolades ('03, '04, '05); in the other season ('02), he was a second-team All-Pro. More impressive, Roaf again made the NFL's all-decade team for the 2000's.

In thirteen NFL seasons, Willie Roaf made the Pro Bowl eleven times.

FOX Sports' columnist Jason Whitlock called Roaf "the second-best offensive tackle of the modern era, finishing just behind Cincinnati left tackle Anthony Munoz."[196] Former Saints' teammate Wayne Martin said of Roaf: "He was the best tackle I played against in the league period. The only guy that I played against that came close to him was Anthony Munoz."[197]

Saints' fellow Hall of Famer Rickey Jackson said Roaf "was the best offensive tackle I played against. He was hard to beat. I always thought he was the best lineman in the game."[198]

On the evening of August 4th, 2012, Willie Roaf was officially inducted into the Hall of Fame. With the entire Saints' team in the audience donning black "77" shirts (Roaf's jersey number), the Saints watched Roaf's induction before playing in the annual Hall of Fame preseason game the following night.

On a proud night for Saints' fans, Sean Payton showed up to the ceremonies as well. Granted permission by the NFL to attend, Payton arrived to support both Roaf and Payton's personal friend Cortez Kennedy, who was also being inducted in the same class with Roaf.

ESPN's Chris Mortensen explained Payton's approved attendance:[199]

> Sean Payton is in Canton, Ohio, after receiving permission from the NFL to attend the Pro Football Hall of Fame induction ceremony and reception. ...Payton can't attend the game, stay in the team hotel or have football-related interaction with his team.
>
> Payton is there to honor former Seattle defensive tackle Cortez Kennedy, who now works as a Saints adviser. Earlier, ESPN reported that Payton was cleared to attend to honor Saints tackle Willie Roaf.
>
> NFL executive vice president of football operations Ray Anderson granted permission for Payton to attend the induction with the aforementioned conditions attached after the coach made the request, league spokesman Greg Aiello confirmed.

The first opportunity for the Saints to have social interaction with Payton will occur at Friday night's Hall of Fame ceremony honoring Roaf, among other inductees. Payton is scheduled to sit at Roaf's table.

Prior to the induction ceremonies, Payton briefly interacted with his Saints' team for the first time since his Goodell-imposed exile in April. Captured by TV networks covering the event, Payton had a brief moment to speak with Drew Brees, Joe Vitt, and the rest of his team before settling in to watch the ceremonies.

Joe Vitt said: "Mr. Benson told [Payton] to go back and say hello to his team. It's the first time I've seen him since April. It was good to see him. It was emotional. He got to say hello to his team."[200]

Regardless of its brevity, a Payton sighting was a welcomed development. In the most abnormal of offseasons, any sign of normalcy -- no matter how short lived -- was a relief.

This wasn't the last appearance by Sean Payton during his suspension, but he wouldn't surface again to see his team for several months.

In the meantime, though, the Saints were fully immersed in preseason preparations in early August. The defense was in the midst of learning a new scheme under defensive coordinator Steve Spagnuolo, and the public was still waiting to learn the identity of the team's interim-interim coach for the first six games of the season.

With the normalcy of football returning, the chaos of Bountygate only intensified. In late July, proceedings in the lawsuits filed by Vilma and the NFLPA had started in New Orleans' federal court.

Judge Helen Ginger Berrigan presided. More twists and turns loomed.

15: holding court

Ten days prior to the Saints' preseason opener at the Hall of Fame game on August 5th, preliminary hearings in the Bountygate case began in federal court in New Orleans under the Honorable Helen "Ginger" Berrigan.

Officially, Judge Berrigan serves in the United States District Court for the Eastern District of Louisiana.

These hearings centered on the accused players' motions to have their suspensions overturned; Jonathan Vilma also sought an injunction that would temporarily place his suspension on-hold until the case's conclusion.

Though Vilma filed a lawsuit separate from the lawsuit the NFLPA filed on behalf of Will Smith, Scott Fujita, and Anthony Hargrove, the suits were eventually consolidated and would be heard as one. Mostly, their goals were the same: the overturning of the suspensions. Because Vilma's suspension was "effective immediately," he filed a motion for an injunction so that he could rehabilitate his injured knee at the Saints' facilities and ultimately practice with the team while the bounty proceedings unfolded.

Because Smith's, Fujita's, and Hargrove's suspensions didn't take effect until week one of the regular season, they weren't (yet) in need of a similar injunction. They were still free to participate in all team activities.

After July 23rd settlement talks between the players and the NFL failed to produce anything meaningful, Jonathan Vilma's first hearing took place on July 26th in Berrigan's chambers. As referenced earlier, Vilma called several witnesses (teammates, coaches, and former teammates) to testify under oath on his behalf and refute the NFL's accusations, specifically the alleged Favre bounty.

In hearing testimony from Saints' employees, NFL attorneys, and Peter Ginsberg, Judge Berrigan weighed the arguments on the merits of the NFL's investigative and sanctioning process as a whole; the contention as to Roger Goodell's jurisdiction to impose discipline; Goodell's ability to serve as an impartial arbitrator; and the conflicting accounts of what the NFL accused the Saints.

On the stand, Joe Vitt again directly denied the Saints ever operated a bounty program. When asked if the Saints maintained a bounty program, Vitt said: "I want you to listen to me hard because I'm going to speak to you soft. No."[201]

While Ginsberg attacked the NFL's process, its evidence, its potential violation of CBA bylaws, and Roger Goodell's alleged pre-judgment of the investigation's outcome, NFL attorneys simply argued that the court did not have jurisdiction to rule on the matter. The league's collective bargaining agreement superseded any outside challenges, they claimed.

During this hearing Judge Berrigan appeared sympathetic to Vilma's case, saying that Goodell's claim that he punished the players for "conduct detrimental" (events that didn't occur on the field of play) "[bordered] on ridiculous."[202]

This is what Judge Berrigan meant, more completely: Goodell claimed the Saints operated a pay-to-injure program, and that Saints' players were financially rewarded for inflicting injuries to targeted opponents on the field.

Goodell then punished the players based on a violation of the Players' Conduct Policy ("conduct detrimental"), which solely governed off-field misconduct. This, Berrigan felt, was "ridiculous." If Goodell had evidence that Saints' players were compensated for injuries inflicted to opponents on the field, then how was that an off-field violation?

Had Goodell ruled the accused players engaged in on-field misconduct, he wouldn't be legally authorized to levy discipline for those transgressions. So in an effort to both levy the discipline and rule on the appeals -- thus solely controlling the outcome -- Goodell needed to employ the "conduct detrimental" route.

Also, this route freed Goodell from having to back up his claims (that Saints' defenders engaged in malicious activity) with video evidence from games played. Because Goodell didn't punish players for on-field violations, the video evidence that proved Saints' defenders did not maliciously and purposefully injure opponents was mostly irrelevant.

As Joe Vitt would say in December when testifying to Paul Tagliabue, referring to the Saints playing within the rules on a weekly basis:[203]

> ... there's nobody in the league office, there's nobody on our officiating crews that would investigate our football team based

on the body of work that's on TV, that's on the field every Sunday. Nobody.

In addition to this, Judge Berrigan added that she had "serious jurisdictional concerns"[204] as to Roger Goodell's authority to impose discipline in this case. As Peter Ginsberg argued that the levying of punishments should have rested with a third party arbitrator because it dealt with alleged on-field misconduct, Berrigan initially seemed to support that idea without officially ruling on it.

In summary, the players argued (in part) that if they were being punished for operating a pay-to-injure system, then that equated to on-field misconduct; that subsequently meant that a third-party arbitrator, and not Roger Goodell, should have determined the suitable discipline. On the other hand, the NFL argued that the players' operation of a pay-to-injure system fell within the nebulous bounds of "conduct detrimental" which thus supported Goodell's authority to impose discipline and rule on the appeals.

Judge Berrigan ended the day's proceedings without ruling on the matter.

The players and the NFL then readied themselves for their next hearing on August 10th.

***

In the days leading up to the August 10th hearing, attorneys for both the players and the NFL initiated a variety of legal filings related to their cases. Again, the fundamental underpinning of this legal action was a dispute on whether the discipline levied for the alleged misconduct should be identified as an on-field transgression (alleged financial rewards for alleged injuring of opponents) or as an off-field violation (conduct detrimental).

If the alleged activity by the players entailed on-field misconduct, then Roger Goodell overstepped his authority and thus, the suspensions would be illegitimate and subsequently voided. This is what the players' lawsuits sought to establish.

On August 4th, Roger Goodell doubled down on his belief that the Saints operated a bounty program. In an interview with reporters in advance of the Hall of Fame game, Goodell said:[205]

> The No. 1 thing is when you reward players for injuring other opponents, that's a bounty. That's not pay for performance, that's a bounty ... anything that would target or reward people for injuring other players, that's not part of football.
>
> When you reward somebody for injuring somebody ... that's not semantics. We also have evidence that players were targeted, as we've indicated to you all and told you.

Regardless of the pushback from the players and the feeble state of the NFL's evidence, Goodell refused to back down or compromise his stance.

To this day, the NFL has never provided evidence that a Saints' opponent was targeted and then injured, and that a Saints' defender was subsequently rewarded for inflicting the injury. The fact is that not even one instance of this alleged target-injure-reward sequence was ever uncovered by the NFL.

Further, in the three seasons the NFL accused the Saints of running an injury program, the league never punished any Saints' player for injuring an opponent on the field of play. And why? Because no opponent was ever injured outside of the accepted, legal framework of the game's rules. If a Saints' opponent was injured, it was an incidental result arising from the natural course of legal play. Revisionist accusations aside, these facts revealed a gaping disparity between what the NFL accused the Saints of engaging in, and what factually occurred on the field of play.

No matter, Roger Goodell was steadfast in his allegations that the Saints operated a bounty program even while his narrative crumbled.

On August 6th, *ESPN's* trio of Chris Mortensen, Adam Schefter, and Ed Werder reported that the NFL offered to reduce Jonathan Vilma's suspension to eight games as part of settlement talks, and in exchange for Vilma dropping his defamation lawsuit against Roger Goodell.[206]

The NFL quickly denied this, but a report three weeks later reaffirmed the validity of the offer. Mike Florio reported:[207]

> Earlier this month, a report emerged that the league had offered to cut Vilma's one-year suspension in half. The NFL denied that any such offer had been made.

Our source, who is in position to know, says it happened. It's still not clear whether it was a formal offer or an implied -- but nonetheless clear -- indication that if Vilma would accept an eight-game reduction an eight-game reduction definitely would be available.

It was a moot point anyway because Vilma wasn't interested in settling the case. He wanted exoneration. The court hearing on August 10th would be the next step in attaining that vindication, and the proceedings inched Bountygate forward.

***

The August 10th hearing before Judge Berrigan included not just Jonathan Vilma, but the other three players as well. While the players argued their case, the NFL argued theirs and also filed a motion to dismiss all of the players' lawsuits.

The crux of the players' argument was this, according to Tulane Sports Law Professor Gabe Feldman:[208]

> The players argued to the court that ... Goodell was biased, he prejudged the outcome of the case, his punishment was arbitrary and capricious, he exceeded the scope of his authority under the terms of the collective bargaining agreement, and he failed to give the players due process.

On the other hand the NFL maintained their same argument from the July 26th hearing. Feldman reported the NFL's stance was that:

> ... federal law and the terms of the collective bargaining agreement simply do not permit a judge to undo or interfere with the commissioner's decision to punish players for conduct detrimental to the league.

Like the July 26th hearing, Judge Berrigan appeared sympathetic to the players' cases. Berrigan, in part, said:[209]

> I would like to rule in Mr. Vilma's favor. I think the proceedings were neither transparent nor fair. I think I made that clear the other day...

> I think the refusal to identify the accusers, much less have them at the hearing to be cross-examined, to look at biases, flaws in their testimony, and 18,000 documents that apparently were

relied upon by Mr. Goodell, less than 200 were actually provided to you, many of them were redacted...

I think you were thwarted at every [turn] by Mr. Goodell's refusal to provide you meaningful access to witnesses and to documents.

This rebuke from a federal judge did not cast a positive light on Goodell's actions, and reaffirmed the players' position that they had been subjected to a flawed process.

Additionally, Judge Berrigan questioned NFL attorneys on Goodell's basis for using "conduct detrimental" as his standard for punishment instead of what she perceived as an Article 14 CBA violation (an on-field violation), which dealt with pay-for-performance non-contract bonuses -- an area outside of Goodell's authority to punish.

After NFL attorney Gregg Levy circuitously explained Goodell's reasoning for basing punishment on "conduct detrimental," Berrigan responded that Goodell "did a complete end around everything."[210] This further reiterated Judge Berrigan's view that Goodell's process was an unfair -- and possibly illegitimate -- one.

No matter, Berrigan concluded the hearing without making a ruling on any of the issues before her. She also suggested the continuation of settlement talks.

Most significantly, she said "I still have serious questions as to whether I can do anything until the August 30th panel makes a ruling."[211]

***

This August 30th panel referred to a separate appeals' process within the Bountygate proceedings. Before Judge Berrigan would intervene from her position and issue a ruling, she presumably felt it was important for the league's internal appeals' process to run its course. While the players were challenging Goodell's authority in federal court, they were simultaneously challenging that authority within the confines of the league's CBA process. It was an attack on dual fronts.

The league's internal CBA process was still ongoing, and this August 30th panel was the next and perhaps final step.

Recall back to the NFLPA's first challenge of Goodell's authority in early May -- the "System Arbitration" filing that ultimately resulted in arbitrator Stephen Burbank upholding Goodell's jurisdiction. Beyond this ruling, the players had the right to challenge Burbank's decision that upheld Goodell's authority.

That happened in an August 30th hearing by a three-person panel consisting of retired federal Judge Fern Smith of San Francisco, retired federal Judge Richard Howell of New York, and Georgetown professor James Oldham.[212]

This panel weighed the issue of whether Goodell was within his authority to punish the players for alleged acts entailing "conduct detrimental," or if the levying of punishments should fall under on-field conduct provisions that were beyond the scope of Goodell's jurisdiction.

The ruling from this panel would be critical, one way or the other.

***

By September 4th, the Tuesday after the Labor Day holiday, the panel had not yet returned a ruling. Timing was of the essence because the NFL season was set to start in full on Sunday, September 9th. Suspensions were slated to start in week one for Fujita, Hargrove, and Smith. Additionally, Judge Berrigan was still yet to rule on Vilma's motion for placing his suspension on-hold so that he could return to the team until the case concluded.

The players, their attorneys, the Saints, and Saints' fans waited anxiously for this ruling.

On Friday September 7th the panel unanimously overturned the players' suspensions, a significant victory for the players. This not only allowed the four players to head into the regular season free from suspensions, it also validated their claims that Roger Goodell wrongly disciplined them.

Goodell had overstepped his authority. Aside from being mildly chastised by Judge Berrigan, Goodell then had a panel of two former judges and one law professor unanimously rule against him. This was a revealing sequence of events.

In overturning the players' suspensions, the panel determined that Goodell's authority for imposing punishment was unclear.

In part the panel's ruling read: [213]

In our view, the alleged bounty program was both an undisclosed agreement to provide compensation to players and an agreement to cause, or attempt to cause injury to opposing players.

Therefore, the System Arbitrator would have exclusive jurisdiction to impose penalties for the undisclosed compensation terms of the bounty program. And the Commissioner would have exclusive jurisdiction to impose penalties for the players' agreement to seek to injure opposing players.

The panel drew a two-part distinction in the allegations: one, that there was an alleged agreement among players to pay each other bonuses; two, that there was an alleged agreement among players to cause injury to opponents.

According to the CBA, Goodell was only within his rights to impose discipline for the second of these two parts, but not the first. Because of the harshness of the penalties and the uncertainty for what Goodell based his ruling, the panel vacated the suspensions.

Though this was a victory for the players, it was not a final ruling because the panel "[remanded] the matter back to the Commissioner for expeditious redetermination."[214] What this meant was that the panel recommended that Goodell clarify his basis for discipline and "redetermine" (i.e., reissue) the punishments quickly.

Essentially, the internal disciplinary process would start over from scratch.

After six months of caustic acrimony and seemingly endless procedural iterations, Goodell and the players were back to square one. Unbelievable.

Almost a week after the panel's ruling, the NFL released a statement that read, in part:[215]

> The panel made clear that the Commissioner had full authority to impose discipline on the players so long as the discipline was attributable to conduct detrimental to the league, rather than "undisclosed compensation."
>
> The panel asked only that he clarify that he was not relying on the "undisclosed" nature of the financial incentives in imposing the discipline. In the meantime, the panel put the suspensions on hold.

Peter Ginsberg responded accordingly:[216]

> It is interesting and illuminating that it took the NFL almost one week to develop a publishable rationalization of the Appeals Board decision.
>
> Contrary to the NFL's media statement, the Appeals Panel voided the suspensions — it did not "put the suspensions on hold," as the NFL now pretends. And the Appeals Board is clearly based on the conclusion that the Commissioner overstepped his jurisdiction.

Regardless, Roger Goodell would be re-issuing discipline in the near future. Heading into the season, though, the players were free and at least temporarily vindicated. Laughably, this process that took six months to rule that Roger Goodell had overstepped and misapplied his authority was now officially back in the hands of Roger Goodell for a new ruling.

A kangaroo court, indeed.

Sports on Earth's Mike Tanier, in an astute analogy, compared Goodell's rule to that of the Roman Empire before the fall.

In part, Tanier expounded on what he called "the circular logic of Goodell making a ruling on Goodell's abuse of power":[217]

> Last Friday, a three-person internal review panel ... ruled to overturn the bounty suspensions commissioner Roger Goodell levied against four former Saints players. The panel decided that since Goodell's case tangentially involved salary-cap violations (the money earned from the alleged bounties represented compensation above and beyond the cap), there was a jurisdictional overlap between Goodell and the system arbiter, Stephen Burbank.
>
> Burbank himself ruled in June that Goodell had the authority to issue the suspensions. And Goodell now reserves the right to review and possibly adjust the suspensions that the panel overturned. Logically, we have crossed the Rubicon. The whole appeals process sounds delightfully Roman...
>
> Goodell allowed the players to probe his governing contraption for weaknesses. They found one. He can now circumvent it until he spackles it up, carefully making sure that his future rulings

avoid mention of the salary cap, and that all salary-cap rulings are issued through Burbank...

The battle over the salary-cap technicality tacitly acknowledges the commissioner's absolute power over other disciplinary matters; questions about whether he had ample evidence to levy the suspensions in the first place have been back-burnered.

And soon, the circular logic of Goodell making a ruling on Goodell's abuse of power will have the awesome legal power of precedent: He can reduce these sentences and gain the absolute power to choose not to next time. It sounds more like a plot point in a swords-and-sandals epic than something that can happen in 21st century America, yet here we are.

The phrase "conduct detrimental to the league" could be interpreted in sweeping ways, and a lot of palace intrigue can be concealed behind the distractions of bread and circuses.

***

By the weekend of September 8th, the Saints were preparing to play their season opener in the Superdome against the Washington Redskins and their highly-touted rookie quarterback, Robert Griffin III. In an offseason consumed with drama, distractions, and discontent, the Saints were finally getting back to football.

Coming off of a 2011 season, one in which the team set a litany of NFL records en route to finishing 13-3, the Saints were ready to build on that success and make a run at being the first team to play in the Super Bowl in their home stadium. If Bountygate hadn't given the team ample motivation, the opportunity to win a Super Bowl title in the Superdome certainly did. As emotional and discouraging as the 2012 offseason had been for fans, the prospect of another successful season temporarily subordinated the offseason's negativity. The season opener on September 9th was a date highly anticipated by Saints' fans. Now that it was here, and now that the accused players in Bountygate had been temporarily vindicated, things were looking up. A novel change.

With Aaron Kromer installed as the Saints interim-interim coach on August 23rd, Joe Vitt and Mickey Loomis were set to depart the team and serve their suspensions. The silver lining of the season's opening weekend still had a bit of grey, especially with the reality that Sean Payton would be absent for the entire season.

With so much having happened through the first eight months of 2012, there was still plenty more to come.

The season was yet to tell its story, and Bountygate was waiting to write its final chapters.

***

Chapter Postscript

For quick reference, here's a glance at the simultaneous challenges the players waged, and where they stand according to the timeline we've followed thus far:

<u>Internal CBA Process</u>

a.) Goodell punishes players; b.) Players challenge his authority under the CBA; c.) Arbitrator upholds Goodell's authority; d.) Players file subsequent appeal to 3-man panel for a final ruling; e.) 3-man panel overturns suspensions, sends case back to Goodell to start over from scratch; f.) ...

<u>Federal Court</u>

a.) Goodell punishes players; b.) Players participate in June 18th appeals' process; c.) Goodell upholds discipline; d.) Players sue in federal court to overturn suspensions; e.) Judge Berrigan conducts hearings, waits to rule until internal CBA process finishes; f.) ...

16: dueling declarations

Week one of the 2012 season did not start, or end, well for the Saints. Heading into week one against the Redskins in the Superdome, the Saints were eight point favorites to win their season opener. The Redskins, though, mostly effortlessly handled the Saints en route to winning 40-32. A 33-17 fourth quarter deficit was too much for the Saints to overcome and they ended week one with a home loss. Coming on the heels of a 2011 season in which the team was 9-0 at the Superdome, the 2012 season was off to an inauspicious start.

After the offseason the team had endured, the loss almost seemed fitting.

Not only did the Saints' new-look defense surrender 40 points, they also allowed 459 yards. Rookie quarterback Robert Griffin III posted a close-to-perfect 139.9 passer rating and ran for 42 yards. It was almost as bad an opening act for the Saints and their defense as imaginable.

Week two in Carolina wasn't any better. For a second consecutive week, the Saints found themselves trailing by double digits in the second half. The defense was a disaster once again, surrendering 35 points and 463 yards, while Panthers' quarterback Cam Newton rushed for 71 yards and registered a 129.2 passer rating. The Saints lost 35-27.

For all the renewed optimism that had come with the beginning of the season, that hope was quickly evaporating in the face of an 0-2 start.

***

The Monday after the Panthers' game, the Bountygate saga took another twist. While Roger Goodell was in the process of redetermining the accused players' punishments after the appeals' panel voided their suspensions, a signed declaration from Gregg Williams leaked to the public.

This declaration explained Williams' role in the Bountygate allegations and clarified Williams' -- and perhaps the NFL's -- explanation of the events in question. What immediately stood out from this declaration was its date: September 14th, 2012.

Exactly a week after the appeals' panel overturned the players' suspensions, the NFL secured a signed declaration from Williams. Whether this was a retroactive move aimed at developing new "evidence" in light of the NFL's increasingly discredited investigation, or whether it was an attempt by the NFL to coerce Williams into relaying official testimony favorable to the league (in order for Williams to gain reinstatement) is up for debate.

What's inarguable is that this supposed key document, one that partly supported a version of events that bolstered the NFL's accusations, did not come into existence until six months after the Bountygate scandal started.

If Williams' testimony was so important to the NFL, it was vexing that it wasn't officially on the record until six months after the fact.

Without an official record available early in the process, how could anyone corroborate what the NFL claimed Williams told them in the prior months? How would anyone know if Williams' September declaration conflicted with statements he made earlier in the process?

Mike Florio of *Pro Football Talk* opined that Peter Ginsberg and NFLPA attorneys would argue the declaration was "procedurally defective," due to the timing of its arrival and its re-opening of the evidence record this deep into the process.[218]

Williams' declaration revealed several things; whether Williams was credible or not was a matter of interpretation. Regardless, here were the key points from Williams' declaration.

In outlining the Saints' pay-for-performance -- not "bounty" and not "pay-to-injure" -- system, Williams explained:[219]

> I decided to take control of the players' pay-for-performance pool ... I personally designed how the pool would work initially, assigned monetary values to on-field performance criteria, held the funds in a box in my office, and administered the pool by awarding financial payouts and assessing amounts due ... Additional funds came from ... on-field mistakes—e.g., penalties...

Describing the terminology he used ("kill the head," "cart off," "knockout," etc.), Williams said:[220]

> I cannot remember the precise difference between a "cart off" and a "knockout," but they were together a category of big hits that resulted in an opposing player leaving the game due to the hit (for example, having the "wind knocked out of him" or being shaken up or injured in some other way) and not returning to the game for one or more plays.

Then apparently contradicting himself later in the declaration, and also refuting some of the NFL's fundamental accusations, Williams said this:[221]

> These terms, documents, and references had absolutely nothing to do with the pay for performance pool, any bounty payments, injuring opposing players, or payments of any kind, and did not violate any league rule.
>
> ... these terms had to do with basic football techniques, strategies, and practices.

In one moment Williams explained how the terms corresponded to rewards under his pay-for-performance system; then a few lines later he said they "had absolutely nothing to with the pay for performance pool." These two conflicting statements were part of the many inconsistencies in the Williams' declaration that cast doubt upon his credibility.

About payment specifics, Williams stated:[222]

> Payments were only made for plays that took place during a game the Saints won, so individual accomplishments were not rewarded unless the overall result was a team victory.
>
> If a penalty was called on a play, no payment would be made for anything that happened on the play. It was a core part of our defensive philosophy that penalties were not acceptable ...
>
> If the player responsible for the penalty was participating in the pool, he would owe money to the pool...

This statement corroborated Scott Shanle's descriptions in June when Shanle explained to *The Times Picayune's* Mike Tripplet that illegal conduct was discouraged under the rules of the Saints' pay-for-performance system. If Saints' defenders were indeed fined for engaging in conduct that incurred a penalty, then why would they seek to maliciously injure their opponents?

The NFL's contention that Saints' players would reward each other for injuries inflicted on opponents made little sense from a financial standpoint on multiple levels. First, it defied logic that a Saints' defender would seek a nominal $500-$1,000 reward when he risked a substantial, five-figure fine from the NFL for maliciously attacking an opponent.

Second, if the Saints' defenders were so indoctrinated by this system, then why would they stray beyond its guidelines and engage in conduct that would cause them to incur fines rather than earn rewards?

This was a simple conflict of logic, one the NFL never addressed.

In line with this reasoning of not incentivizing and rewarding malicious conduct, Williams declared:[223]

> It was my view and intention that we were only encouraging clean, aggressive hits within the rules of the NFL ... we did not intend to incentivize and did not make payments ... for illegal hits or on-field misconduct.
>
> While I understand that the pool payments were prohibited by the NFL rules, they were not payments intended to reward on-field misconduct.

After Williams explained that his program did not reward players for on-field misconduct, he explicitly stated he never advocated the injuring of opponents. Specifically, Williams stated:[224]

> I now understand that it is possible that rewarding ... a substantial cash payment could encourage players to injure opposing players.
>
> At the time, while I knew that conduct violated league rules, it was never my intent to cause our opponents to be injured...

It was difficult to reconcile this statement with the Pamphilon audio from January of 2012. If you recall, Sean Pamphilon captured Williams saying this (among other things) prior to the Saints-49ers January 2012 playoff game:[225]

> We need to decide if Crabtree wants to be a fake ass primadonna, or if he wants to be a tough guy. We need to find it out. He becomes human when we fuckin' take out that outside ACL.

Though the Saints' defenders didn't heed Williams' exhortations in that game (the Saints incurred zero penalties), Williams' pre-game speech clearly conflicted with what he testified to in his declaration. And once again, this lent credence to the unreliability of Williams' testimony.

Which words were true, which were false, which were hyperbole, and which were made out of desperation and self-preservation? Any way one looked at the situation, it was difficult to wholeheartedly believe Gregg Williams.

When it came time to make an official statement on the alleged Favre bounty, Williams stated in his declaration:[226]

> During a team meeting the night before the 2009 NFC Championship Game ... Mr. Vilma addressed the defensive players and coaches (including me) who were present and pledged $10,000 to any player who knocked Brett Favre out of the game...

> After Vilma spoke, the situation escalated and a number of others present pledged additional amounts (I do not recall specific identities or amounts) to the pay-for-performance pool ... those additional pledged amounts were never given to me ...

Of Williams' claim that Vilma offered a $10,000 bounty on Favre, perhaps the most important question is this: why did the first official record of Williams' indictment of Vilma come six months after Bountygate arrived? Did Williams make this claim in the previous months? Did his testimony ever change? How would anyone know one way or the other?

More important, how does one weigh Williams' claims against those of the eight individuals who testified under oath in federal court that Vilma did not offer this bounty?

Should one believe the claim of just one person, one who's shown a clear pattern of inconsistency and unreliability, one who's likely desperate to acquiesce to the NFL in order to resume his career, all without having to submit his testimony under oath in court?

Or should one believe the testimonies of eight different individuals who denied the claim in front of a federal judge, all at the risk of perjuring themselves and potentially serving jail time?

Which side seemed more reasonable to believe?

Finally, Williams' declaration relayed this bit of information that would eventually fall short of its implications:[227]

> When I was interviewed, I personally misled NFL investigators by denying knowledge that anyone associated with the Saints had made any commitment or pledge that a player who knocked Brett Favre out of the game would be entitled to payment.

According to this nearly incomprehensible sentence from Williams, he initially "misled" NFL investigators about Saints' players pledging and being "entitled to payment" for knocking Brett Favre from the game. In other words, when NFL investigators first asked Williams if players pledged and were entitled money related to the Favre bounty, he said no. In September of 2012, Williams then said Saints' players did pledge money and were entitled to a reward.

But by December 2012 -- as we'll see -- when testifying in front of Paul Tagliabue, Williams would once again alter this testimony in relation to the Favre bounty. Yet again, the consistently conflicting nature of Williams' statements cast him as anything but a reliable witness. No matter, the NFL championed Williams as a credible source.

In three months, Williams would finally testify and subject himself to cross-examination from the accused players' attorneys. Further clarification awaited; but for now, this September 14th declaration was the only record of Williams' claims.

When Mike Cerullo's declaration leaked a day later (September 18th), the claims of the NFL's other primary source became public. Though it seemed clear the NFL was leaking this testimony in an effort to bolster their case before re-issuing player discipline, Cerullo's declaration was rife with inconsistencies and faulty claims.

***

On Tuesday, September 18th the NFL leaked Mike Cerullo's declaration, outlining Cerullo's allegations and role in Bountygate.

Unlike the Gregg Williams' declaration that arrived soon after the players' suspensions had been overturned, Cerullo's declaration was signed and dated months earlier: May 22nd, 2012.

But like the date on Williams' declaration, the date of Cerullo's was also suspect. First of all, as was becoming a pattern with the NFL's evidence, this document that was supposedly vital to the NFL's case did not come into existence until after Bountygate arrived; after the coaches were disciplined; and after the players were punished.

The failure to have Cerullo's claims in an official record prior to the dispensing of sanctions was troublesome because he was the NFL's primary source. For months the NFL touted the allegations and contentions from Cerullo as the basis of their investigation, but never possessed an official record of his testimony until well after the fact.

What this meant, essentially, was that the NFL could claim Cerullo said any number of things that were to their liking, all without having to support those claims with any documentation.

It was a case of the NFL saying that a person said some things, from which the NFL then levied damning accusations and historic punishments. This was a paper-thin standard. When the accused players attacked the NFL for a lack of due process, this is partly to what they were referring.

Though Cerullo contacted the NFL via email in November 2011 about the bounty claims[228] -- strangely, nearly two years after the alleged events in question -- the NFL failed to produce an official record of his testimony until more than six months after his initial statements to them.

Cerullo's November 2011 email to NFL's spokesman Greg Aiello read:[229]

> So I have info on Saints Joe Vitt Lying to your NFL Investigators on Bounties from 2010, along with proof!!! I was there, in the cover up meetings, with players and Joe, I love the NFL and want to work there again, but I am afraid if I tell thge [sic] truth I will never coach again in NFL, But I was fired for a situation that the Saints encourage.
>
> All I want is a Job back in the NFL as a QC Coach anywhere, so If talking to you jepodizes [sic] that I will have to get back to you, but The Saints are a Dirty Organization. Contact me.

According to the NFL, this email -- rife with spelling errors, smacking of ulterior motive, polluted with vitriol, and reeking of questionable rationality -- supposedly re-opened the league's bounty investigation that started during the 2010 offseason.

Equally troubling was the NFL's initial claim that Cerullo came to them with "significant and credible new information ... during the latter part of the 2011 season."[230]

If Cerullo had been gone from the Saints since April 2010, how would he possess "credible new" information seventeen months after he'd last set foot in Saints' facilities? Even if this information was simply "new" to the NFL, how would Cerullo's claims legitimately establish a bounty program during two seasons Cerullo wasn't even a Saints' employee?

With consideration to Cerullo's poor history with the Saints, it was unreasonable to think that a Saints' employee was feeding second-hand information to Cerullo in the seasons after he was fired.

"Credible new information" from Mike Cerullo seemed like a stretch.

Anyway, why would Cerullo finally deliver these claims to the NFL in November 2011? There are no answers beyond speculation, but the fact that Cerullo had been fired in April 2010 and didn't surface with damning allegations until seventeen months later was a curious circumstance. Did Cerullo slow-burn for a year-and-a-half until he finally contacted the NFL? Or did the NFL seek out Cerullo in an effort to proactively build a case against the Saints, and encourage him to email his accusations?

It was likely one or the other, but the time gap was nonetheless confounding.

Either way, the NFL didn't secure an official record of Cerullo's statements until May 22nd, 2012. This was (conveniently?) less than a week after Jonathan Vilma sued Roger Goodell for defamation. Perhaps fearful that this lawsuit exposed Goodell for having made incriminating public comments about Vilma's involvement without documentation supporting those accusations, the NFL may have scrambled to document Cerullo's claims to prove Goodell possessed a basis for his comments.

***

Here were the key parts of Cerullo's May 22nd, 2012 declaration:

Like Williams, Cerullo referred to the Saints' program as a "pay-for-performance" and "defensive performance program," not a "bounty" or "pay-to-injure" program.[231]

Cerullo reiterated that the Saints' pay-for-performance system discouraged plays that incurred penalties. He also corroborated Williams' statement that Williams handled all the money involved. Cerullo said:[232]

> The fines for poor performance were sometimes called "vaginal donations." All cash collected for the program was stored in a lockbox in Mr. Williams' office.

Centrally, Cerullo claimed Jonathan Vilma pledged a $10,000 bounty on both Kurt Warner and Brett Favre during the 2009-'10 playoffs. Of the alleged Warner bounty, Cerullo claimed:[233]

> In the NFC divisional playoffs, the Saints faced the Arizona Cardinals. During a meeting of the defense the night before the game in January 2010, Jonathan Vilma, a Saints defensive captain, asked for permission to address the team, which was granted.
>
> Mr. Vilma, in the course of giving a motivational speech to the team, stated, while raising his hands, each of which held stacks of bills, that he had "two five stacks" (which I understood to mean $10,000) for anyone who knocked Cardinals quarterback Kurt Warner out of the game.
>
> I personally collected the money that Mr. Vilma left on the table at the front of the room and subsequently gave it to Mr. Williams for safekeeping.

This statement from Cerullo was populated with a series of outright lies and inconsistencies. At the time of this declaration's release, the falsehoods were unverified as such; not until Cerullo testified in front of Paul Tagliabue in December would Cerullo admit to their inauthenticity.

Equally important, Cerullo's claim of a bounty on Warner didn't align with Gregg Williams' declaration. Williams claimed Vilma pledged a bounty on Favre, but made no mention of a bounty on Warner. As Peter Ginsberg outlined in a legal brief:[234]

Even former Saints defensive coordinator Williams, the mastermind of the alleged Bounty Program, does not contend that Vilma put a bounty on Warner.

As the NFL's only two sources on these alleged bounties, one source established in detail the allegations of a bounty on Warner, while the other source made no reference to it whatsoever. Either Cerullo falsified this claim or Williams purposely omitted it. One way or the other, these conflicting accounts damned the credibility of these men's testimonies.

More revealing, Cerullo claimed he "personally collected" the $10,000 Vilma pledged on Warner and "gave it to Mr. Williams for safekeeping." Yet Williams, in his declaration, clearly stated "I was never given any money by anyone because of a pledge related to an injury of a particular player."

Yet again, inconsistency reigned. Did Cerullo or did he not collect the money? Did Williams or did he not take the money for safekeeping? One of these two principal sources was not telling the truth.

Cerullo continued in his declaration to make the same bounty allegation related to Brett Favre:[235]

> At a defensive meeting the Saturday prior to that Sunday game, after Mr. Williams had addressed the team, Mr. Vilma said, in substance, that his prior offer of $10,000 for knocking out the quarterback "still stands" for any player who knocked Brett Favre out of the game.

Cerullo tellingly employed the phrase "in substance" to characterize Vilma's words. He did this because he could not recall what Vilma actually said, nor did he have any record of Vilma's words. Cerullo was making a damning accusation from an event 28 months prior without any documentation to support his claims.

It was a tacit admission that he did not recall exactly what happened. "In substance," rather than verified fact, was a dubious standard when careers and reputations were on the line.

Also in his declaration, Cerullo stated that Gregg Williams instructed him to "get rid of documents that referenced the pay-for-performance" program[236] and that Joe Vitt followed up to ensure Cerullo deleted the files.

There was a disconnect between the NFL's claims of 18,000 incriminating documents totaling 50,000 pages, and Cerullo's claim that he destroyed critical evidence. If he destroyed it, what exactly did the NFL gather that outlined the Saints' program? Or was Cerullo being untruthful when he made this claim?

When questioned during cross-examination about whether Cerullo destroyed evidence as instructed, Joe Vitt responded with equal parts sarcasm and clarity:[237]

> ... You know, I felt such strong trust with Mike Cerullo, especially after the last four weeks he missed work, that I could really trust in him, that I could tell him the deep down secrets of my heart, let's destroy these documents. Mike, just me and you because we're tight.
>
> No. The answer is no. Cerullo is an idiot.
>
> ... I mean, what are we missing? The NFL told me that they have ... 50,000 pages and 18,000 documents. So what could we possibly be missing?

***

A key characteristic reinforced by the release of these two declarations was the fragility and unreliability of the NFL's official record of evidence.

Because Cerullo and Williams were the two sources incriminating the Saints, it was essential for the NFL to have their claims on an official, verified record early in the process -- and before the issuing of sanctions. But that wasn't the case.

Instead of an official record of statements dictating the disciplinary process, unverified claims -- according to only the NFL -- formulated the basis for punishments.

Because many of the NFL's claims failed to hold up under scrutiny, it was critical for official documentation to exist as a foundation for the league's allegations and sanctions. But official records of these declarations, perhaps tailored specifically to fit the NFL's narrative, did not come into existence until well after the fact, and until after most of the damage had been done.

It was a standard that lacked merit and a commitment to the truth.

***

With the official accounts from the NFL's primary sources now in the public record, Roger Goodell would soon re-issue discipline to the players. Bountygate was reincarnating into its second self.

Meanwhile, the Saints were struggling on the field. The absence of Sean Payton, Joe Vitt, and Mickey Loomis was clearly evident, and the Saints' 2012 team -- which at one point early in the year held such promise -- appeared to be a shell of its once formidable self.

It wasn't all for naught, though. The Saints were set to play their first primetime game of the season in early October.

A gentle reprieve from the chaos was on its way.

17: a historic night

By week five of the season, the Saints were 0-4.

Against Kansas City in week three, the Saints squandered a 24-6 lead deep in the third quarter -- in the Superdome -- and lost 27-24. Chiefs' runningback Jamaal Charles racked up an ungodly 288 yards of offense, including a 91-yard touchdown run. The Saints' defense surrendered an embarrassing 510 yards to a team that would ultimately post an NFL-worst 2-14 record in 2012.

In week four at Green Bay, the Saints lost 28-27 to a desperate Packers' team. This time, the Saints failed to protect a fourth quarter lead. The critical sequence in the game came with seven minutes remaining and the Saints trailing by a point. Darren Sproles dropped a routine pass on 3rd and four, resulting in a Garrett Hartley field goal attempt. Hartley nailed the 43-yard kick to temporarily put the Saints ahead 30-28, but a penalty negated the kick and Hartley subsequently missed his next try. Shortly thereafter, the Saints lost their fourth straight game of the season.

Through four weeks almost everything had gone wrong for the Saints on the field, and the game-altering sequence late in the game against Green Bay was representative of the 2012 season to date.

Not since 2007 had a Saints' season started so poorly.

**

In week five, the Saints hosted the San Diego Chargers in the *NBC* Sunday Night Game of the Week. It was the Saints' first primetime game of the season, a time slot in which the team enjoyed much success during the Sean Payton era.

More significant, Drew Brees was poised to set the NFL record for touchdowns thrown in consecutive games, a hallowed 52-year old record under the ownership of the great Johnny Unitas.

With 2:58 left in the first quarter Brees broke the record when he threw a 40-yard touchdown to Devery Henderson, Brees' 48th-consecutive regular season game with a touchdown pass. Another significant NFL record now belonged to Brees.

In several games during Brees' steak, Brees threw just one touchdown pass. Brees, though, came no closer to losing his streak than he did in week eight of the 2011 season. Against the St. Louis Rams, Brees threw a "meaningless" touchdown to Lance Moore with just six seconds remaining in a game the Saints lost by ten points.

That pass extended the streak Brees initiated in week five of the 2009 season against the New York Giants. Brees' crowning moment in eclipsing Unitas' record then came against the San Diego Chargers, Brees' former team who years' prior had discarded him in favor of Philip Rivers.

With Devery Henderson catching the historic pass, Henderson too further cemented his legacy in Louisiana football lore. In 2002 while playing for LSU, Henderson caught one of the most famous touchdown passes in NCAA history, a play termed the "Bluegrass Miracle." In that game, with LSU trailing the University of Kentucky 31-27 in Lexington, LSU possessed the ball at its own 26-yard line with just two seconds remaining.

On the game's final play, LSU quarterback Marcus Randall heaved the ball downfield to a blazing Henderson, one of the NCAA's fastest wide receivers. In a stroke of luck, a Kentucky defender deflected the ball toward his own end zone -- catapulting the ball farther downfield -- and a streaking Henderson ran underneath the tip, caught the ball in stride, and sprinted into the end zone for the game-winning touchdown. LSU won the game 33-31 in what play-by-play announcer Dave Neal called "the most shocking, improbable, unbelievable sequence of events."[238]

With his historic catch from Brees, Henderson now possessed two of the most famous catches in Louisiana football history.

Brees and Henderson, though, weren't the only two Saints' players who made history against the Chargers.

Saints' wide receiver Marques Colston caught his 50th and 51st career touchdown passes as a Saint, surpassing the franchise record set by Joe Horn from 2000 - 2006. Colston -- a Saints' fan favorite, a seeming afterthought of a draft pick in the seventh round of 2006, and one of the NFL's toughest, most humble, most consistently productive, most vexingly-underrated wide receivers -- now stood alone as the most decorated wide receiver in Saints' history seven years into his career.

On a night where Brees deservedly received the lionshare of the recognition, Colston earned his too.

While the records fell by the wayside, Sean Payton, Joe Vitt, and Mickey Loomis were in the building to see it all happen. With all three men still serving their suspensions, Drew Brees made an official request to the league seeking permission for them to attend the game. The NFL granted Brees' request.

Though Brees certainly hoped that Payton, Vitt, and Loomis would be present to experience the potentially record-setting night in the confines of their home stadium, there was perhaps an ulterior motive to Brees' request.

A week earlier, the NFL had granted Gregg Williams permission to attend the St. Louis Rams – Seattle Seahawks game. As the suspended defensive coordinator of the Rams, Williams -- for whatever reason -- attended this game on approval from the NFL.

Mike Florio of *Pro Football Talk* explained the significance:[239]

> It was horribly misguided to let Williams attend a game, especially after he gave a sworn statement implicating Saints linebacker Jonathan Vilma as offering $10,000 to anyone who knocked former Vikings quarterback Brett Favre out of the 2009 NFC title game. To erase the appearance of preferential treatment, the NFL had to extend a similar courtesy to the other folks who have been suspended.
>
> It's possible, if not probable, that Brees made the request not because he wants them there, but because he knows in his capacity as a member of the NFLPA Executive Committee that a rejection would have helped the cause of the players who face re-issued bounty suspensions, particularly Vilma.
>
> Even with permission granted, the handling of Williams' situation justifies suspicion regarding some sort of a quid pro quo...

Even with a historic night on tap in the lead-up to the Sunday night game, even with the reassuring presences of the suspended Saints' management in the building, Bountygate continued to cast its ominous shadow over the league and the team.

The Saints ultimately beat the Chargers 31-24, and secured their first win of the season headed into the bye week. However remote, the hopes of a winning steak and a return to contention lingered. All wasn't lost just yet.

Soon Roger Goodell would again flex his authority in the Bountygate scandal. And like the first time, the accused players wouldn't react favorably to Goodell's decisions.

18: "a big sham"

Fewer than 48 hours after the Saints beat the Chargers, Roger Goodell announced his amended discipline to the accused players in Bountygate.

Goodell provided window dressing in the form of minor reductions to the penalties, but more importantly protected his authority by clearly defining the reasoning behind his decisions.

With Goodell now having stated that he punished the players exclusively for "conduct detrimental," he was free from outside interference. With this reissuing of discipline, it was a foregone conclusion that the players would appeal Goodell's ruling -- yet again.

Because of this conduct detrimental clarification, Roger Goodell positioned himself to once again preside over the next appeals' hearing. For a process supposedly aimed at providing due process and impartiality, this circular meandering that continued to lead back to Goodell was farcical.

For those scoring at home, the internal CBA process unfolded like this from the start:

May 2: Goodell disciplines the accused players

June 5: Special Master Stephen Burbank upholds Goodell's jurisdiction

June 18: Players appeal to Goodell; Goodell upholds punishments

September 7: Secondary appeals' panel voids suspensions due to Goodell's misapplication of his authority; panel recommends a "redetermination," which basically resets the entire process

October 9: Goodell re-rules on his violation of jurisdiction, in essence getting a mulligan for overstepping his bounds; Goodell reissues player discipline accordingly

The official statement from the NFL on the reissuing of player discipline read:[240]

> Commissioner Roger Goodell reaffirmed the discipline for four players in the New Orleans Saints' bounty matter today, but

adjusted certain aspects of it following recent meetings with each of the players ...

Commissioner Goodell clarified that his decision was based entirely on his finding that the bounty program represented conduct detrimental to the league and professional football. The Saints' bounty program operated over a three-year period and offered incentives to players for plays including "cartoffs" and "knock-outs," which were plays that caused injuries to opponents.

Though the NFL's original statement on Bountygate referenced player violations for offering "non-contract bonuses,"[241] this updated ruling eliminated that allegation as a basis for Goodell's sanctions. These "non-contract bonuses" -- the money rewarded under the Saints' pay-for-performance program -- fell outside of Goodell's jurisdiction; as a result Goodell decided the foundation for his new sanctions was unrelated to these payments.

In order to solely rule on the issue, Goodell now based the punishments "entirely" on conduct detrimental to the NFL, whatever that might have entailed. What it did mean, peripherally, was that the NFL did not discipline the accused for any on-field misconduct. "Conduct detrimental" exclusively referred to off-field violations.

Again, this was an admission that there was no on-field activity to punish. Had there been, it strained believability to think the NFL would not have disciplined Saints' players for engaging in malice and misconduct on the field of play.

Still, Roger Goodell maintained his reference to a multi-year bounty program, which was a distortion of terminology and facts. A three-year "bounty" program suggested that Saints' defenders were routinely targeting opponents, proactively assigning cash rewards for injuries inflicted, and then maliciously injuring targeted opponents to gain said reward.

This distortion was far from the truth, but the "bounty" terminology enabled Goodell to maintain his established narrative: that he was punishing a rogue franchise of ill intent in an effort to ensure player safety. Perpetuating this narrative -- faulty or not -- seemed to be of the utmost importance to Goodell.

Equally important, Roger Goodell altered his claims in this new ruling to more passively reference "incentives ... for plays that caused injuries to opponents." This was crucial.

The NFL's original statement[242] alleged, in a much more active and specific tone, "'bounty' payments to players for inflicting injuries." This intimated a premeditated targeting, a purposeful infliction of injury, and a verified financial reward for the completion of the act.

Where it was first "players ... inflicting injuries," it was now "plays that caused injuries." Where it was first "bounty payments," it was now "incentives." This new version was much less specific and it enabled Goodell to fit his accusations into the loosely-defined "conduct detrimental" category.

"Payments" indicated verifiable cash transactions. "Incentives" had no inherent relation to financial rewards and, as such, required no empirical evidence to prove their existence. Was hyperbole and pre-game banter now considered an "incentive" too?

"Players ... inflicting injuries" suggested video evidence of Saints' defenders harming opponents. When no on-field video corroborated that accusation, the NFL morphed their allegation to "plays that caused injuries." In virtually every NFL game, plays naturally result in injury from legal events. That's a much different circumstance than players purposefully "inflicting" injuries.

In short, when Goodell failed to produce evidence that supported his initial claims of "players ... inflicting injuries" and "bounty payments" rewarded for those alleged injuries, he morphed his allegations into the realm of the nebulous to both preserve his authority and maintain his original accusation.

Now according to Goodell, the establishment of a *potential* incentive for a legal play (not a cash transaction, nor a suspected on-field transgression) was "conduct detrimental." This apparently represented what Goodell continued to call a "bounty program."

***

On Scott Fujita's amended discipline, Roger Goodell reduced Fujita's suspension from three games to one. Goodell cited Fujita's failure to eliminate the pay-for-performance program from the Saints' locker room. Goodell ruled:[243]

> I am surprised and disappointed by the fact that you ... ignored such a program and permitted it to continue.

> Your failure to act contributed to allowing this program to remain in place not only during the 2009 season, but for two additional seasons after that.

Ridiculously, Goodell claimed Fujita should have personally dissolved the program and because he didn't, the Saints' pay-for-performance system continued to operate during the 2010 and 2011 seasons when Fujita wasn't even on the team. Of all the absurdities involved in Bountygate, this might have been the most absurd of all.

For Anthony Hargrove, Goodell reduced his suspension from eight games to seven, with credit for five games served. Goodell maintained his stance that Hargrove...[244]

> ... engaged in conduct detrimental by falsely denying ... both the existence of the Saints' program and the pledge of a substantial payment to any member of the Saints' defensive unit who knocked Brett Favre out of the 2009 NFC Championship Game...
>
> The existence of the program has been admitted by numerous Saints coaches and players ... And, based on substantial evidence, ... I have found that a member of the Saints defensive unit made such a pledge with respect to Mr. Favre.

Even though Hargrove, in his declaration, clearly denied knowledge of a bounty program and a bounty on Favre, Goodell simply decided this was a false denial because it refuted Goodell's claim. And though Goodell stated the program's existence was "admitted by numerous Saints coaches and players," he failed to clarify that the admissions were of a pay-for-performance program that rewarded legal plays in games the Saints won, and not a bounty program that targeted opponents for injury on a routine basis.

This distinction was crucial to the truth, yet Roger Goodell refused to differentiate the realities in an effort to distort the circumstances to his liking.

Further, Goodell speciously ruled that because he believed someone pledged a bounty on Favre, Hargrove knew about it and then lied to NFL investigators. This was an inference rooted in conjecture and draped with faulty logic. Even if the facts proved a bounty on Favre (they didn't), it still did not logically follow that Hargrove was conclusively aware of it. When Hargrove denied the NFL's claims, Goodell decided Hargrove was lying and punished him accordingly.

On Will Smith, Goodell ruled[245] there was no change to Smith's suspension, and that Smith's alleged contributions to the Saints' program -- both financial and organizational -- justified the upholding of a multi-game suspension. Though Smith denied assisting in the establishment of the program and further denied that there was ever an intent to inflict injury, Goodell disregarded Smith's testimony.

In amending Jonathan Vilma's sanctions, Goodell upheld Vilma's season-long suspension but allowed Vilma to collect salary for the six weeks of the 2012 season Vilma spent on the "physically unable to perform" list while rehabbing a knee injury.

More specifically, Goodell ruled:[246]

> At our meeting, you confirmed that cart-offs and knockouts were part of a broader program in place among the Saints' defensive players. You confirmed that these terms referred to plays in which an opposing player has to leave the game for one or more plays.
>
> I also find that you engaged in conduct detrimental by offering a substantial financial incentive to any member of the defensive unit who knocked Brett Favre out of the Saints' 2009 NFC playoff game against the Vikings. (There is also credible evidence that you made a similar pledge regarding Kurt Warner in the immediately preceding playoff game against the Cardinals, but whether you made multiple pledges of that kind does not matter for purposes of the discipline that I have decided to impose.)
>
> I have personally met with both [Mike Cerullo and Gregg Williams] and have had an opportunity to assess their credibility. I am not persuaded by any suggestion that either Mr. Williams or Mr. Cerullo had an incentive to testify falsely...

Perhaps the most revealing facet of this ruling was Goodell's contention that the claims from Mike Cerullo and Gregg Williams were "credible" and that, by extension, the sworn testimony in federal court by eight Saints' employees was not.

ESPN's Andrew Brandt summed up Goodell's amended discipline like this: "Although there is some relief here, primarily financial for Vilma ($570,000) and Fujita ($429,000), this is more of the same."[247]

Window dressing, indeed.

***

As was protocol by now, the NFLPA quickly issued a response. About the reaffirmed sanctions, the NFLPA stated:[248]

> For more than six months, the NFL has ignored the facts, abused the process outlined in our collective bargaining agreement and failed to produce evidence that the players intended to injure anyone, ever. The only evidence that exists is the League's gross violation of fair due process, transparency and impartiality during this process.
>
> Truth and fairness have been the casualties of the league's refusal to admit that it might have made a mistake. We will review this decision thoroughly and review all options to protect our players' rights with vigilance.

The NFLPA was not alone in its criticisms to the sanctions. Peter Ginsberg, Vilma's attorney, responded accordingly.[249] Ginsberg accused Goodell of attempting to "fit a square peg into a round hole" when shoehorning the league's allegations under the "conduct detrimental" umbrella. Ginsberg further chastised Goodell for failing to "fairly and impartially evaluate the evidence."

Lastly, Ginsberg said this:

> Someone needs to tell the Commissioner directly that his duties also include being true to the evidence, to fundamental notions of due process and to the integrity of the game...
>
> Jonathan Vilma did not offer a bounty or any incentive to any teammate to injure an opposing player. Commissioner Goodell has now called every one of the ... players and coaches a "liar" ... who has sworn under oath to that fact.

When the attorneys finished responding, Drew Brees and Scott Fujita made public statements too.

In two separate media appearances,[250] Brees said Goodell based the Bountygate accusations and punishments on "speculation and rhetoric and ... the testimony of some pretty unreliable sources."

Brees then finished by saying:

> This whole bounty thing, for the most part, is just a big sham. The fact that our coaches are suspended for part of the year or the entire year is pretty ridiculous.

Not to be outdone, Scott Fujita issued a pointed statement directed specifically at Roger Goodell. In full, it read:[251]

> I'm pleased the Commissioner has finally acknowledged that I never participated in any so-called "bounty" program, as I've said for the past 7 months. However, his condescending tone was neither accurate nor productive. Additionally, I am now purportedly being suspended for failing to confront my former defensive coordinator for his inappropriate use of language. This seems like an extremely desperate attempt to punish me. I also think it sets a bad precedent when players can be disciplined for not challenging the behavior of their superiors.
>
> This is an absolute abuse of the power that's been afforded to the Commissioner.
>
> For me, the issue of player health & safety is personal. For the league and the Commissioner, it's about perception & liability.
>
> The Commissioner says he is disappointed in me. The truth is, I'm disappointed in him. His positions on player health and safety since a 2009 congressional hearing on concussions have been inconsistent at best. He failed to acknowledge a link between concussions & post-career brain disease, pushed for an 18-game regular season, committed to a full season of Thursday night games, has continually challenged players' rights to file workers compensation claims for on-the-job injuries, and he employed incompetent replacement officials for the start of the 2012 season. His actions or lack thereof are by the league's own definition, "conduct detrimental".
>
> My track record on the issue of player health & safety speaks for itself. And clearly, as I just listed, the Commissioner's does too.

***

In an effort to keep the league's owners abreast of the developments, and perhaps lobby them on the validity of the allegations and sanctions, Roger Goodell issued a "Report on Further Proceedings in Bounty Matter (October 9th, 2012)" to all 32 teams.

In this report, Goodell reiterated that his discipline fell entirely within the bounds of conduct detrimental to the league. Goodell then repeated a series of accusations in his "Summary of Evidence" that were not consistent with facts, logic, or responses from the parties involved.

About Cerullo coming forward in late 2011, Goodell said:[252]

> During the latter part of the 2011 season, we received substantial new information, including documentary evidence, that showed: (i) that a sophisticated and pervasive bounty program had been in place at the Saints during the 2009 through 2011 seasons; and (ii) that a specific bounty had been placed on Mr. Favre during the playoffs following the 2009 season. Upon receipt of this new information, we reopened our earlier investigation.

As discussed previously, because Mike Cerullo was fired in April 2010, it strained credulity to believe that he supplied the NFL with "substantial new information" that confirmed the existence of a "pervasive bounty program" during two seasons that Cerullo was not a Saints' employee.

It was one thing to claim that Cerullo provided information related to the alleged Favre bounty because, after all, Cerullo was a Saints' employee at the time. But for Cerullo to possess credible information that established a "pervasive" program in the years after he'd been fired was illogical, if not downright ludicrous.

Also in his "Summary of Evidence," Goodell cited four different scenarios that supposedly served as conclusive proof of this bounty program. Goodell's first citation was this:

> ... in a game between the Saints and the New York Giants in 2009, a Saints player earned a reward for a cartoff of Giants running back Brandon Jacobs, who left the game with a shoulder injury.

According to the NFL's official play-by-play,[253] Brandon Jacobs was injured on a clean, unpenalized hit midway through the 2nd quarter. Jacobs later returned to the game and played for its remainder. More importantly, Goodell provided no evidence that a member of the Saints put a bounty on Jacobs -- remember, this was supposedly a "pervasive bounty program" -- nor did Goodell identify the Saints' player allegedly rewarded for this play.

In prior months, Goodell attempted to claim Saints' safety Roman Harper received a $1,000 reward during this game. Goodell tenuously tried to connect that alleged reward to the legal hit on Jacobs, but the problem was that Darren Sharper tackled Jacobs -- legally -- on the play Jacobs was temporarily sidelined.

This is why Goodell didn't identify in this latest report who offered and who received a reward for that alleged "cartoff." There was no proof that a bounty was pledged or that a cash transaction ever occurred, only a flimsy intimation that it happened.

Goodell's other three citations of Saints' defenders being rewarded for inflicting injuries came from a Saints-Panthers game in 2010. As you remember, the NFL first claimed these three rewards were a result of the Saints-Bills game in 2009. When that was shown false, Goodell amended the accusation and claimed it was the Saints-Panthers game in November 2009. Soon that was proven false also.

By October, Goodell now claimed these three financial rewards happened in November 2010 during the Saints-Panthers game. This is how Goodell described it in his October 9th report:[254]

> In that game, three Carolina players were seriously injured: running backs Jonathan Stewart and Tyrell Sutton, who were literally carted off the field with a head/neck and ankle injury, respectively, and quarterback Matt Moore, who was later placed on injured reserve, unable to return for the remainder of the season, with a torn labrum.

Again, these three injuries all occurred within the routine course of accepted play and none of the three plays involved a penalty or otherwise malicious conduct. They were all legal plays.[255] Further, Goodell provided no evidence that the Saints placed bounties on Stewart, Sutton, or Moore, nor did he reveal any details related to financial transactions associated with these events.

Goodell did nothing more here than share the fact that three players got hurt in a game against the Saints.

Of these three plays, there was no proof that a Saints' defender was ever rewarded for incidentally injuring these men while making a legal tackle. Had there been proof, Roger Goodell wouldn't have faultily identified three separate games where rewards for these alleged "cartoffs" occurred. Had there been proof, it seemed logical the NFL would have uncovered it in its 50,000 pages of documentation verified by forensic experts.

Like the Jacobs' citation, these claims fell far short of the NFL's accusation that Saints' players targeted and maliciously injured opponents for financial rewards.

Most important is this fact: over the course of the three seasons that the Saints supposedly operated this pervasive bounty program, the Saints' defense participated in 3,382 total plays (regular and post seasons). The NFL identified only four plays that they believed supported their accusations.

That represented a miniscule .12% of total plays the Saints' defense played. How was that pervasive?

Not only were these four cited plays routine in light of what occurs on an NFL field weekly, they were all legal plays -- never penalized by officials during the games, never resulting in league fines the week following those games. Nor was there evidence supporting premeditated bounties, nor evidence revealing cash transactions. Yet according to Roger Goodell, this was conclusive proof of a highly-organized, multi-year bounty program that justified, among other things, Sean Payton being suspended for an entire season.

Finally, as discussed earlier, Roger Goodell identified Jimmy Kennedy -- a former Minnesota Vikings player -- as an individual who confirmed the Favre bounty. This is how Goodell positioned it in his October 9th report's "Summary of Evidence": [256]

> Brad Childress, then Head Coach of the Minnesota Vikings, informed us that he believed that Saints players had placed a bounty on Vikings quarterback Brett Favre.
>
> In subsequent discussions, Coach Childress said that a Vikings player, Jimmy Kennedy, had told him that the Saints defensive unit had offered a $10,000 bounty on Mr. Favre and that Mr. Kennedy had identified Anthony Hargrove, then a defensive player for the Saints, as the source of his information.
>
> Our office promptly investigated this matter. We interviewed Coach Childress and Mr. Kennedy.

As we know, Kennedy vociferously denied this claim and issued a statement in response. He said:[257]

> Roger Goodell identifies me as the whistleblower who approached former Viking coach Brad Childress about an alleged

bounty on Brett Favre in the NFC Championship game. That is a lie. I had no knowledge about any alleged bounty to reveal to anyone, and I never informed anyone that I did...

Roger Goodell also states that I was interviewed by the NFL about the alleged bounty. That is another lie; I was never interviewed by the NFL, unless the NFL considers two 30-second conversations when I told NFL Security that I had no knowledge of any such allegations interviews.

The NFL states that Anthony Hargrove told me about the alleged bounty on Brett Favre. That is an utter lie; it simply never happened. I never discussed an alleged bounty with Anthony Hargrove before, during or after the NFC Championship game.

If Goodell's reissuing of the sanctions was aimed at appeasing the players, mending severed relations, establishing a believable set of events, and moving forward with a fair resolution, it fell spectacularly short.

On the other hand, if Goodell's goal was to prove himself intractable, then he succeeded admirably.

One way or the other, this ruling only further inflamed the tensions between the accused players, the Saints, and Roger Goodell. Bountygate was a festering, open wound.

Another appeals' hearing was on deck.

***

With the NFL nearing the heart of its regular season and Bountygate still stealing headlines, Roger Goodell would finally capitulate and seek outside assistance in an effort to resolve the lingering acrimony poisoning the Bountygate proceedings.

In the meantime, Joe Vitt was set to return from suspension and assume interim head coaching duties. The Saints were about to re-establish their winning ways and the playoffs weren't yet out of the question.

And while Saints fans settled into the enjoyment of a winning streak, they would soon be cold-cocked by yet another maddening revelation.

19: a recusal, a revelation, and a rivalry

Ten days after Roger Goodell reissued discipline against the accused players, he recused himself from presiding over their upcoming appeals' hearing. Considering Goodell's apparent desire to solely control the Bountygate proceedings, this was a surprising move.

By recusing himself, Goodell allowed another individual to preside over and rule on the players' next (and final) appeals' hearing. Empowered by the league's collective bargaining agreement to appoint a third party to arbitrate, Goodell handed the Bountygate reins to former NFL Commissioner Paul Tagliabue.

After NFLPA Executive Director De Smith released the news via Twitter, *Pro Football Talk's* Mike Florio reported:[258]

> The announcement came from NFLPA executive director DeMaurice Smith on Twitter. Per Smith, Goodell will hand the baton to former Commissioner Paul Tagliabue. It's a power the Commissioner possesses under the Collective Bargaining Agreement. And Smith got advance notice because the CBA requires Goodell to consult with the NFLPA.

Goodell indicated that his appointment of Tagliabue was designed to "bring the matter to a prompt and fair conclusion."[259] Additionally Goodell relayed that he would have no role in Tagliabue's upcoming hearing, and that at no point during the Bountygate saga had he discussed the case, or otherwise consulted, with Tagliabue.

As the hearing officer, Paul Tagliabue possessed "full authority and complete independence" to make a final ruling.

Though Tagliabue's appointment was a positive development for the players, it wasn't without an asterisk. In what was potentially a conflict of interest, Tagliabue worked for the law firm that represented the NFL in both of the Bountygate-related lawsuits currently in federal court.

Peter Ginsberg explained the significance:[260]

> The commissioner's decision today makes it clear to us that he's finally been convinced there is no way he could ever have been a fair and neutral arbitrator.

Having said that, we need time to evaluate whether Commissioner Tagliabue—as much as we respect the work he did for the NFL—is an appropriate replacement given the fact Mr. Tagliabue works for the same law firm representing Mr. Goodell in both the challenge to the discipline, as well as Mr. Vilma's defamation lawsuit against Mr. Goodell.

The fear, obviously, was that Tagliabue's impartiality would be compromised. As the thinking went, instead of presiding fairly over the matter, Tagliabue would potentially rubberstamp Goodell's sanctions in order to lend the process an air of legitimacy. Moreover, were this to happen, it would likely protect Roger Goodell legally -- an outcome of particular importance to Tagliabue's employer.

After the manner in which the NFL had clumsily and improperly handled Bountygate thus far, this wasn't an irrational fear. Regardless, any replacement for Roger Goodell at this point seemed like an improvement.

Largely praised for his efforts in ensuring the Saints remained in New Orleans in the aftermath of Hurricane Katrina, Paul Tagliabue was a trusted source and his appointment seemed to be an olive branch of sorts. If there was an individual capable of placating the situation and restoring faith in the process -- especially among Saints' fans -- Tagliabue was among the best candidates.

Though there was no official indication as to why Goodell recused himself, the arrival of Tagliabue signaled, perhaps, a desire on the part of the league's owners to solve the Bountygate conundrum that had riddled the league for much of the 2012 calendar year.

With the NFL descending on New Orleans for the Super Bowl within four months, it was perhaps in the NFL's best interests to mend relations with the Saints, their fans, and the city itself. An unwelcoming city wouldn't be an ideal destination for the NFL's premier annual event, one covered by thousands of media outlets and watched by millions of people worldwide.

By this interpretation, the NFL was sending Paul Tagliabue to the rescue.

Tagliabue, though, wouldn't be without a challenge of his own before the appeals even started.

***

The Sunday following Tagliabue's appointment, the Saints played at Tampa Bay. In one of the more entertaining games of the season, the Saints won 35-28 to bring their record to 2-4. A penalty against the Buccaneers erased a tying touchdown on the game's final play, and the Saints avoided blowing a 14-point fourth quarter lead.

During a 19-minute stretch in which the Saints' offense scored five touchdowns, Saints' fans caught a glimpse of the record-setting 2011 offense that, for much of that season, effortlessly dominated opposing defenses.

Moreover, two of the Saints' most memorable plays of the season came during this game. In one, Malcolm Jenkins chased down the Bucs' Vincent Jackson on Jackson's 95-yard catch-and-run, tackling Jackson at the Saints' one-yard line. The Saints' defense converted this play into a goal-line stand that proved to be the difference in the game's outcome.

In the other play Saints' wide receiver Joe Morgan caught an acrobatic 48-yard touchdown, a play in which he caught the pass; flipped a charging Bucs' defender over his back; juked a second Bucs' defender; and then dove into the end zone while simultaneously colliding with a third Bucs' defensive back in the vicinity.

It was one of the NFL's signature touchdowns of the season.

***

The next week, a hurricane intervened.

With the players' appeals set for October 30th, Hurricane Sandy decided to extend the Bountygate drama a bit longer. On October 27th, Paul Tagliabue officially postponed the hearings with Hurricane Sandy bearing down on the NFL's corporate office on the east coast.

For the NFL and Roger Goodell, this wasn't the only storm on the horizon.

Coupled with the hearings' postponement was an NFLPA motion in federal court to have Tagliabue removed as the hearing officer for these appeals.

Because of Tagliabue's employment at the law firm representing the NFL, the players' union decided that this conflict of interest prevented Tagliabue from being an impartial arbitrator. Though Judge Berrigan --

whose court presided over the Bountygate litigation -- was under no mandate to rule on the motion, the NFLPA filed it nonetheless.

Paul Tagliabue would respond in short order.

***

On October 28th, the day after Tagliabue postponed the Bountygate appeals, the Broncos trounced the Saints 34-14 in Denver in Joe Vitt's first game back from suspension. Playing in the nationally-televised Sunday Night Game of the Week, the Saints submitted one of their worst performances of the season.

The defense surrendered 530 yards, including 225 yards rushing. The offense converted only one of twelve third down opportunities and the team fell to a dispiriting 2-5.

In his postgame press conference, Joe Vitt referred to the team's repeated defensive breakdowns as "catastrophic."[261]

Through seven games, the reengineered Saints' defense under Steve Spagnuolo was on a dubious pace to shatter the NFL record for most yards surrendered in a season. At what was almost the season's midway point, any hope for defensive improvement was fading fast.

***

Eight days later, the events of November 5th were bizarre and action-packed.

Paul Tagliabue informed the NFLPA he would remain in place as the hearing officer for the upcoming appeals; the Saints played the Philadelphia Eagles in a nationally-televised Monday night game; and Saints' fans learned, shockingly, that Sean Payton's contract extension -- signed in September 2011 -- was voided by the NFL, meaning that Payton would no longer be under contract with the Saints at season's end.

In a calendar year that never failed to produce drama, the first week of November indicated that the madness of 2012 wasn't quite yet ready to end.

As reported by *ESPN's* Chris Mortensen[262] on Monday, November 5th, Paul Tagliabue rejected the NFLPA's argument of partiality and denied their request that he recuse himself for the upcoming appeals. With Judge Berrigan not ruling on the NFLPA's motion to dismiss

Tagliabue as the arbitrator, Tagliabue moved forward and scheduled the appeals' hearing for November 20th.

Bountygate was nearing its final lap.

That same night, the Saints hosted the Eagles on Monday Night Football. The Saints won the game handily 28-13, improving their record to 3-5. The defense posted a season-high seven sacks, with second-year defensive end Cameron Jordan submitting a career-best performance of three sacks, five quarterback hits, and two tackles for losses.

At the same time, the defense surrendered 221 yards rushing on 7.6 yards per carry. While the Saints had won three of their last four games, the defense continued to struggle.

Neither the Saints' victory nor the news of Tagliabue's refusal to recuse himself emerged as the day's top headline, however. Midday on November 5th, *ESPN's* Adam Schefter reported this:[263]

> Within the past year, the multiyear contract extension the Saints announced for Sean Payton in September 2011 was voided by the NFL, making the suspended head coach a free agent after this season and casting questions on how long he will remain in New Orleans, according to league sources.

This revelation blindsided Saints' fans. With 2012 appearing increasingly like a lost season, the future of the Sean Payton era in New Orleans was now too suddenly in doubt.

In September of 2011, the Saints and Sean Payton agreed to a five-year contract extension. *The Times Picayune* reported the development:[264]

> The terms of Payton's deal, which will run through the 2015 season, were not disclosed. However, it is believed to have propelled him into the top salary ranks of the NFL coaching fraternity...
>
> Payton's extension should also lay to rest speculation that arose in the off-season about his long-term intentions when it was revealed he had bought a mansion in suburban Dallas and his family was moving there. Though Payton did his best to tamp down fears among Saints fans ... there were still rumblings

among the Saints faithful that Payton had one eye on the Cowboys' job.

Unbeknownst to the pubic, and perhaps even insiders, the NFL rejected this contract extension as submitted. Fourteen months after the news of Payton's new deal came the news that it wasn't a new deal, after all. The timing of this development, and the extended timeframe involved, was odd.

Schefter reported:[265]

> Just as Payton's role in the bounty scandal has been an ongoing saga with the NFL for the past year, so has his contract...
>
> At issue in the contract was one specific clause that would have enabled Payton to walk away from the deal if general manager Mickey Loomis was suspended, fired or left the New Orleans organization...
>
> The league believed that any such language in Payton's contract would set a bad precedent for other coaching contracts and rejected the deal...

The overarching question was this: why did the NFL take so long to make this decision?

It was just one clause, after all. Clouding the issue, there was no official indication of when Sean Payton and the Saints first became aware of the unsuitability of the contract. Was it during the 2011 season, when there would have been ample time to restructure the deal? Or did Payton not officially learn about it until March of 2012 when he was no longer in a position to renegotiate due to his pending suspension?

Schefter included this nugget in his report:[266]

> As recently as March, when Payton was visiting NFL offices to appeal his yearlong suspension in the bounty scandal, he asked NFL commissioner Roger Goodell for the status of his contract extension and was told it was unsatisfactory as it initially was constituted...

This reeked of a potentially extortionary tactic on the part of the NFL. If it was indeed one simple clause that altered the viability of the contract, why did it take the NFL seven months (from September 2011 to March 2012) to inform the Saints and Payton of their decision to reject the deal?

Were Roger Goodell and the NFL squatting on the contract intentionally? More directly, were they planning to leverage a vulnerable Payton into going along with the Bountygate allegations? By March of 2012, Payton was banished from the NFL for a year; he was now without the security of a long-term contract; his current contract was expiring at the end of 2012, when he would still be suspended; and he would ultimately be dependent on Roger Goodell for reinstatement.

Roger Goodell and the NFL had painted Sean Payton into an unenviable corner. It appeared that Payton's predicament was not just one of circumstance, but perhaps one of planning and execution by the NFL.

If this was a viable interpretation, wouldn't it suggest that Bountygate was perhaps set into motion prior to Mike Cerullo's November 2011 email that supposedly reopened the NFL's investigation?

It was a curious set of circumstances, and the timing involved seemed almost diabolical.

***

With fan outrage reignited over the Payton contract fiasco, the week of November 5th was about to get even more interesting.

The Atlanta Falcons, the Saints' longtime division rival and chief nemesis, were coming to town undefeated and owners of the NFL's best record at 8-0.

For the next few days, everything else took a back seat.

20: peak and valley

In the five weeks after the news of Sean Payton's voided contract was made public, the Saints' season flashed an ephemeral hope then burned out in a spectacular fashion.

After the Saints beat the Eagles on Monday Night Football to climb to 3-5, the 8-0 Atlanta Falcons headed to New Orleans for a division showdown. The Saints-Falcons rivalry, though unheralded nationally, is one of the NFL's best-established feuds and the November 11th match-up would add to the rivalry's lore.

Leading up to this game, the Saints were 10-2 in their last twelve games versus the Falcons since Sean Payton and Drew Brees arrived in New Orleans. While the Saints clearly owned the upper hand in the rivalry's recent meetings, the Falcons maintained a level of competence that garnered them respect, if not from the Saints, then from some of the NFL's self-appointed pundits.

Under the coach-quarterback tandem of Mike Smith and Matt Ryan, the Falcons had recently established themselves as consistent yearly contenders for the postseason tournament. Their 0-3 postseason record during the Smith-Ryan era, however, cast doubt on their ability to be true contenders.

In 2012, intent on shedding this label, the Falcons stormed out of the gate undefeated in their first eight games, hopeful to materialize their championship aspirations. Overcoming the Saints in the Superdome would be a key building block for Atlanta's ascension.

Absent their head coach, wallowing in the mire of a nearly year-long malaise, the Saints were seemingly at their most vulnerable point when the Falcons came to town on November 11th. The Saints, though, were ready for the challenge and the Falcons reverted to their recent habit of coming up small in big moments. The Saints handed the Falcons their first loss of the season, emerging with a 31-27 victory.

Saints' running back Chris Ivory, finally installed into the lineup, notched perhaps the team's play of the year on a first quarter 56-yard touchdown run in which he ran around and past an uninterested Asante Samuel before then seeking out and stiff-arming an overmatched Dunta Robinson on his way to the end zone. This touchdown amplified the ferocity of an already fierce home crowd, and the Saints continued their domination of the Falcons and, equally important, moved to 4-5 after an 0-4 start.

For a year devoid of much promise, the flickering hope of the Saints climbing back into contention seemed bright at the moment. Adding to the promise, the Saints arrived in Oakland the following week and bludgeoned the Raiders 38-17 to get back to the .500 mark with six games to play.

After winning five of six games to get to 5-5, the Saints were officially back in the hunt for a playoff spot. With a critical upcoming three-game stretch against division leaders San Francisco, Atlanta, and the New York Giants, the Saints held the keys to their postseason fate in 2012.

Winter was coming.

***

On November 25th the San Francisco 49ers arrived in New Orleans for a key midseason game. Not only did the Saints have an opportunity to further their postseason hopes, they would also gauge themselves against one of the league's best teams. There was also the matter of quieting the ghosts of their January divisional playoff game in San Francisco, a loss that still seemed to haunt the franchise.

With an opportunity for the Saints to move past that painful loss, with the team playing at its highest level of the 2012 season, and with the 49ers' second-year quarterback Colin Kaepernick making only his second career start, the Saints seemed poised for a breakthrough.

The first half of the game unfolded in the Saints' favor, with the Saints holding a 14-7 lead and maintaining control of the game's tempo for much of the half. It all came apart, though, when Drew Brees threw a mindlessly fatal interception that the 49ers returned for a touchdown with just twenty two seconds remaining in the half.

That touchdown tied the score at 14-14, and upon later introspection, it appeared that the Saints didn't recover from that dagger for weeks.

The 49ers proceeded to score two more touchdowns within the first three-and-a-half minutes of the third quarter, with one of those touchdowns coming on another Brees' interception. In the span of fewer than four minutes of game time, the Saints turned a 14-7 lead into a 28-14 deficit.

It was too big of a hurdle to overcome and the Saints lost 31-21.

***

Just four days later, the Saints arrived in Atlanta for a Thursday night game against the Falcons.

On a short week, coming on the heels of a disappointing result against one of the league's most physical teams, the Saints -- and more specifically, Drew Brees -- imploded in a manner foreign to the Payton-era Saints.

The Saints fell into a 17-0 hole before scoring a late first half touchdown to temporarily close the gap to 17-14. An offensive pass interference penalty on Jimmy Graham, however, nullified that touchdown. Two plays later, Drew Brees badly mismanaged the clock and the Saints came away with no points on a drive that ended at the Falcons' three-yard line as the first half expired.

It was a sequence that encapsulated the season's shortcomings, and illustrated the Saints' substandard execution without Sean Payton.

The 17-7 first half deficit ended in a 23-13 loss, a game in which Brees threw five interceptions during a performance that resulted in a career-worst 37.6 passer rating. Adding insult to insult, Brees failed to thrown a touchdown pass, ending his historic streak at 54 games.

It appeared that all of the pressures of 2012 -- the expectations and hindrances and distractions -- overwhelmed Brees all at once and he shattered into a million pieces on national television. It was a performance as stunning and unexpected as it was bad. And it would take Brees and the Saints a few weeks to recover. At 5-7, the Saints' postseason hopes had all but vanished.

The next week in New York would remove all doubt.

***

By late on December 9th, the Saints' season was essentially over. After losing to the New York Giants 52-27 in New York, the Saints fell to 5-8.

Against the Giants, the Saints surrendered a ghastly average of 47.6 yards per return on six kickoffs; the Giants racked up over 300 return yards to go along with nearly 400 offensive yards. Add in the ten Saints' penalties and the Saints had submitted their sloppiest, most apathetic performance of the season.

It was a resounding thud to a three-game losing streak that eliminated the Saints from the 2012 postseason.

On top of that, Saints' cornerback Elbert Mack and defensive coordinator Steve Spagnuolo engaged in a sideline argument -- a rare occurrence for the Payton-era Saints. The episode was perhaps a window into a discontent that portended larger issues with the Saints' defense.

***

With the Saints preparing to play out the string, Bountygate was about to write its final chapter.

Weeks prior, on November 20th, Paul Tagliabue commenced his appeals' hearing. On December 11th, two days after the Saints lost to the Giants, Tagliabue issued his ruling.

For a saga laced with intrigue, ambiguity, and serpentine twists, the final chapter of Bountygate wouldn't disappoint.

21: the tagliabue ruling

On Tuesday December 11th, Paul Tagliabue released his ruling from the players' appeals hearing. This was the final hearing from the nearly year-long saga, and with this ruling the Bountygate case would soon be finished.

The initial news of Tagliabue's ruling came from NFL Spokesman Greg Aiello, who released details of the decision in piecemeal via Twitter. This was an annoying, and perhaps cynical, choice. Instead of first releasing Tagliabue's memorandum in full, Aiello leaked Tagliabue's findings in small doses in an apparent effort to more favorably shape the message prior to the rulings' full release.

This was a last, desperate attempt by the NFL to maintain control of an issue they'd long since lost the ability to control. Because Tagliabue's ruling was a clear victory for the players, Aiello presumably sought to mitigate the damage.

In short Tagliabue voided the players' sanctions in full, but also (confusingly) affirmed Roger Goodell's "factual findings."[267] This conflicting statement presented confusion as it seemingly supported Goodell, yet at the same time exonerated the players.

For months, Goodell argued that these "factual findings" revealed that Saints' players "enthusiastically embraced" a bounty program for inflicting injuries. If those findings were true, consistent with Goodell's public contentions, and validated by Tagliabue's hearing, then it seemed odd that Paul Tagliabue would void the sanctions and refrain from issuing any amended discipline whatsoever.

Was Tagliabue overturning the entirety of the discipline if the accused players truly embraced malicious conduct aimed at injuring opponents? Or were Goodell's factual findings much less damning than he publicly characterized them to be?

What seemed likely was that Tagliabue supported Goodell's findings of a program in place, but this program was largely a benign pay-for-performance system common throughout the NFL. Examination of Tagliabue's ruling and available transcripts (as we'll see) supported this interpretation, and his decision to void all discipline further bolstered this reasoning.

Pro Football Talk's Mike Florio opined after Tagliabue's ruling:[268]

> The fact that the league, which always seems to get to do whatever it wants to do, ultimately didn't enforce a suspension of any kind on any player means that the players won in blowout fashion.

What mattered, for the most part, was Tagliabue's deed: his voiding of all discipline. Had Tagliabue found and truly believed that Saints' players engaged in such malevolent conduct as alleged, it strained belief that he would not have punished them -- even in a much less severe fashion -- for their purported misdeeds.

Instead, he let them walk free and laid blame at the doorstep of the Saints' organization for fostering an environment that, theoretically, could have resulted in injuries to opponents.

Complete analysis of Tagliabue's ruling proved insightful and shed light on Tagliabue's decision-making process and the realities of the events in question. Moreover, Tagliabue illustrated where Roger Goodell and the NFL erred in their process and decisions.

It was a revealing ruling.

In outlining his findings, Tagliabue clarified the basis of the investigation and its allegations:[269]

> The [previously] imposed discipline was the result of the National Football League's investigation of allegations concerning a pay-for-performance program (the "Program") conducted by the Saints during the 2009 through 2011 seasons to reward particular plays by Saints' defensive players that ultimately incentivized rendering opposing players unable to play, and allegations concerning a specific bounty being placed on Brett Favre to injure him during the NFC Championship game against the Minnesota Vikings in January 2010.

What stood out from Tagliabue's description was his use of the term "pay-for-performance program," as opposed to what Roger Goodell continued to disingenuously label a "pervasive bounty program."

Equally important, Tagliabue noted an allegation of only one "specific bounty" where previously Goodell accused the Saints of pledging bounties on Brett Favre, Kurt Warner, Aaron Rodgers, and Cam Newton. What Goodell originally positioned as a multi-year bounty program for the routine infliction of injuries, and the associated targeting of several high-profile quarterbacks, had now -- rightly and factually -- been established as a pay-for-performance program that rewarded legal plays, with an additional allegation of *one* bounty.

After months of distortions and faulty claims, Tagliabue's official record finally clarified the reality of the situation.

In conducting his review and hearing Tagliabue noted, importantly, that he did not review Goodell's "findings and conclusions *de novo*."[270] This meant that Tagliabue did not start the investigation from scratch, but rather relied on the existing record of evidence in making his ruling.

Tagliabue supplemented the existing record with new information to reach his conclusions. Though he affirmed Goodell's factual findings, Tagliabue did so without the benefit of conducting his own investigation. He simply used new material -- witness testimony, mostly -- and compared it to the existing record in order to make a decision. Though time and resources likely prevented Tagliabue from starting a new investigation, his blanket affirmation of Goodell's factual findings would have been much more credible had he done so.

The reliance upon an existing record rife with inconsistencies (the Williams and Cerullo declarations), shifting accusations (the bounty ledger "cartoffs"), and disputed claims (like Jimmy Kennedy's, among others) seemed like a dubious standard.

Nonetheless, Tagliabue indicated that he reviewed the discipline for "consistency of treatment, uniformity of standards for parties similarly situated and patent unfairness or selectivity."[271] His findings, of course, revealed that Goodell applied selective enforcement of an arbitrary standard, inconsistent with precedent. While not directly rebuking Goodell, Tagliabue tacitly admonished Goodell for his erroneous ways.

Tagliabue stated that Goodell's discipline was "seen as selective, ad hoc or inconsistent."[272] Tagliabue's final ruling on each player didn't seem to dispute that notion.

Of Anthony Hargrove, Tagliabue called Hargrove's seven-game suspension "unprecedented and unwarranted."[273] In voiding Hargrove's suspension, Tagliabue ruled:

As a further complication, it is unclear exactly what NFL investigators asked Hargrove regarding the Program or any other alleged program and, thus, unclear whether he lied about the Program or the fact that it included cart-offs and knockouts.

There is evidence in the appeals record that NFL investigators may not have asked Hargrove whether the Saints employed any particular program.

I have concluded that there is not sufficient evidence to demonstrate in these unique circumstances that Anthony Hargrove's alleged misconduct is deserving of a suspension. I therefore vacate the suspension imposed on Hargrove.

As noted previously, where the NFL repeatedly accused Hargrove of obstructing their investigation, Tagliabue found that it was "unclear" what Hargrove had even been asked. Further, there existed exculpatory evidence that indicated the NFL's questioning of Hargrove wasn't related to any program at all.

In the end, Tagliabue found insufficient evidence of what he ultimately called Hargrove's "alleged misconduct" and thus overturned Hargrove's suspension.

In fully exonerating Scott Fujita of any misconduct, Tagliabue found "the NFL's contentions lacking in merit."[274]

He called Fujita's non-participation in the Saints' pay-for-performance program "undisputed"; cited Goodell for levying "inconsistent treatment"; and ruled, in vacating Fujita's suspension, that Fujita's "actions here were not conduct detrimental."[275]

For Will Smith, Tagliabue cited Goodell's "singling Smith out for discipline" as an "inappropriate" act.[276] Tagliabue called Goodell's decision to punish Smith "selective enforcement" that violated "basic requirements" for consistency and fairness when applying discipline.[277]

Because Will Smith, according to Tagliabue, did not engage in behavior any different from many of his teammates, Goodell's decision to discipline Smith simply because Smith was a veteran team leader was a flawed decision.

As a result, Tagliabue voided Smith's suspension.

In his assessment and ruling on Jonathan Vilma and the allegations of the Favre bounty, Tagliabue noted:[278]

> With regard to the alleged bounty, the record on appeal is sharply contested, with witnesses pro and con testifying confidently and with evident contempt for the contrary testimony of other witnesses.

The four individuals who testified on the alleged Favre bounty were Gregg Williams, Mike Cerullo, Jonathan Vilma, and Joe Vitt. Vilma and Vitt, both refuting the allegations, previously testified under oath in federal court. Neither Williams nor Cerullo did. This was important enough that Tagliabue specifically noted it in his ruling.

He stated that Williams and Cerullo "had not been subject to cross-examination in Commissioner Goodell's proceedings or in federal court,"[279] while Vilma and Vitt "both unequivocally testified in the hearing (and in the U.S. District Court for the Eastern District of Louisiana) that Vilma ... did not place a bounty on Favre."[280]

In assessing the credibility of competing testimonies, these facts were highly relevant.

Tagliabue revealed that Gregg Williams, under cross examination, "maintained that Vilma offered the bounty on Favre,"[281] reaffirming the claim Williams made months earlier in his declaration. Williams further testified, according to Tagliabue, that "[Williams] had often previously expressed the view that it was acceptable to strive to knock opposing players out of games."[282]

Williams, though, later undermined both of those claims during the cross exam. Of the alleged Favre bounty, "Williams described it as 'air' or 'funny money' or 'banter'."[283] He then claimed Vilma had "been made a scapegoat."[284] Then, conflicting with his previous statements expressing the acceptability of knocking out opposing players, Williams stated: "You know, at no time, you know, are we looking to try to end anybody's career."[285]

Williams then told Tagliabue that the NFL's investigation was "somewhat of a witch hunt."[286]

Later during his testimony, Gregg Williams (absurdly) blamed Joe Vitt for the years-long existence of the Saints' pay-for-performance program. An *Associated Press* report on the hearings' transcripts included this laughable claim:[287]

> Gregg Williams testified that he tried to shut down the team's bounty system when the NFL began investigating but was overruled by interim Saints head coach Joe Vitt...

Not only was Vitt a defensive subordinate to Williams as the team's linebackers' coach, it was apparently common knowledge in the Saints' organization that Gregg Williams operated with total autonomy, even independent of oversight from Sean Payton.

During his 2011 - 2012 travels with the Saints, Sean Pamphilon learned of this from Saints' players:[288]

> I was told by a couple of Saints players that Williams' contract had a "Fuck you clause," as he used to tell his players. This meant he had complete autonomy and was in absolute charge of the defense.

As was characteristic of Williams' claims by now, it was nearly impossible to know what to believe and what not to believe. The only common trait in his statements was a clear lack of a consistent message. The fact that Goodell -- or anyone for that matter -- would consider Williams' testimony beyond reproach and worthy of the extreme punishments bordered on absurdity.

Under his own cross examination, Mike Cerullo explained to Paul Tagliabue his reasons for coming forward with allegations in November of 2011. Cerullo stated:[289]

> I was angry for being let go from the Saints.
>
> I was angry at Joe Vitt, and I wanted to show that I was fired for lying and I witnessed Joe Vitt lying and he still had a job. So, that was my goal of reaching out to the NFL.

After establishing his reasons for levying the allegations, Cerullo then managed to contradict much of his earlier testimony. In his May 22nd declaration, Cerullo had testified that he "personally collected the money that Mr. Vilma left on the table"[290] prior to the Saints-Cardinals playoff game in January of 2010.

But during his cross exam in front of Paul Tagliabue, Cerullo admitted that wasn't true. This is how the *Associated Press* reported the development:[291]

> Cerullo testified that league investigators misrepresented what he told them, and that, during the playoffs following the 2009 regular

season, he kept track of large playoff pledges on note pads but didn't collect the money.

When questioned about his re-creation -- two years after the fact -- of the handwritten note that allegedly detailed a large bounty on Brett Favre, Cerullo admitted that his claims were "inaccurate" and that he didn't "know what [he] was trying to do with [the] document."[292]

Regardless of the unreliability of both Williams and Cerullo, Tagliabue ruled:[293]

> Evaluating the totality of the evidence, there is an insufficient basis to reject Commissioner Goodell's findings on the offer of the Favre bounty. Commissioner Goodell met with the four principal witnesses in person and made a judgment that Williams and Cerullo were credible witnesses to the alleged bounty offered by Vilma.
>
> In the appeal hearings, despite various inconsistencies illustrated in the cross examination of Williams and Cerullo, neither witness was shown to be not credible on the specific issue of whether Vilma offered a bounty on Favre.

Though Tagliabue noted that the evidence "supported"[294] Goodell's findings of a bounty, he refused to say that the evidence "proved" anything. Tagliabue also consistently referred to the bounty as "alleged" for the entirety of his ruling, even after reviewing all the information available.

In his final ruling on Vilma, Tagliabue said in part:[295]

> It is essential to recognize that Vilma is being most severely disciplined for "talk" or speech at a team meeting on the evening before the Saints-Vikings game. He is not being punished for his performance on the field and, indeed, none of the discipline of any player here relates to on-field conduct...
>
> If one were to punish certain off-field talk in locker rooms, meeting rooms, hotel rooms or elsewhere without applying a rigorous standard that separated real threats or "bounties" from rhetoric and exaggeration, it would open a field of inquiry that would lead nowhere...
>
> ... there is little evidence of the tone of any talk about a bounty before the Vikings game. Was any bounty pledged serious? Was

it inspirational only? Was it typical "trash talk" that occurs regularly before and during games? The parties presented no clear answers. No witness could confirm whether Vilma had any money in his hands as he spoke; no evidence was presented that $10,000 was available to him for purposes of paying a bounty or otherwise.

There was no evidence that Vilma or anyone else paid any money to any player for any bounty-related hit on an opposing player in the Vikings game.

Tagliabue's interpretation seemed to be that there wasn't "clear" evidence of a bounty on Favre and that even if there was, Tagliabue would be incapable of determining whether it was a "serious" pledge or just "trash talk." The record of evidence, simply, failed to prove the accusation.

Tagliabue's voiding of Vilma's suspension, combined with his decision to levy no discipline whatsoever to Vilma, was the strongest of Tagliabue's actions. This was revelatory of an evidence record far less damning than Roger Goodell first characterized, and a final commentary on Goodell's misguided decisions.

Tagliabue then concluded his rulings on the players by stating:[296]

> For the reasons set forth in this Final Decision on Appeal, I affirm the factual findings of Commissioner Goodell; I conclude that Hargrove, Smith, and Vilma engaged in "conduct detrimental to the integrity of, and public confidence in, the game of professional football"; and I vacate all player discipline.

***

While Tagliabue's memorandum provided a comprehensive ruling on each accused player, it also assigned blame to the Saints' coaches and management for the events of Bountygate.

In his ruling, Tagliabue cited the Saints for "broad organizational misconduct"[297] and stated that he "strongly condemn[ed] the misconduct of the Saints' coaches."[298]

This was the crux of Tagliabue's ruling, one that allowed him to protect Goodell (his employer's client) from Vilma's defamation claims and exonerate the players simultaneously. Simply, had Tagliabue overruled Goodell without affirming his findings, he could have exposed Goodell for defaming Vilma. Instead, Tagliabue walked a fine line and held the Saints, not the players, responsible for the off-field misconduct associated with Goodell's "factual findings."

This misconduct entailed, apparently, two things: 1) the establishment of a program that could have yielded -- yet didn't -- an intent to injure opponents; and 2) an obstruction by the Saints' coaches into the league's investigation of the team's pay-for-performance program and the alleged Favre bounty.

Tagliabue called the Saints' pay-for-performance program "deeply misguided"[299] and further ruled that the "entire case ha[d] been contaminated by the coaches and others in the Saints' organization."[300] This claim of "contamination" was difficult to reconcile because it indicated that any refutation or denial by a Saints' employee amounted to misconduct.

When the NFL accused the Saints of intending to inflict injuries on opponents, and the Saints subsequently denied those claims, how did that contaminate the process? If the NFL truly had reams of evidence that indicated the Saints were guilty of what they were initially accused -- specifically, institutionalizing an injury program over three seasons -- then denials and obfuscations would not stand up to the league's supposedly overwhelming evidence.

This claim of contamination seemed to be a red herring, one solely aimed at establishing wrongdoing. Moosedenied, a popular Saints' blog, explained the significance:[301]

> The substance of [Tagliabue's] ruling seems to strongly indicate that what the Saints were actually guilty of wasn't really anything like what Roger would have had us believe.
>
> They can insist that the Saints organization "contaminated the process" by refusing to just admit to whatever charges Roger felt like dropping on 'em. But since when are simple denials capable of "contaminating" anything? It either happened the way you say it did or it didn't. You can either prove it or you can't...
>
> What "contaminated the process" was the Saints' refusal to sacrifice their own reputations by conceding wildly-inaccurate details of the fairy tale Roger had concocted.

The fact that Tagliabue failed to explicitly define how the Saints "contaminated the process" diluted the significance of his claim.

Presumably, Tagliabue intimated that through denials and obstructions, the Saints undermined the league's efforts to investigate. And while the Saints might have done this, those actions did not alter the reality of the team's performance program or the allegations of a bounty on Favre. These were separate issues that Tagliabue conflated in an effort to validate his ruling of culpability.

That nebulous claim, though, opposed the clarity of Tagliabue's ruling on the Saints' pregame meetings, presentation slides, and motivational tactics. On this, Tagliabue stated:[302]

> The conduct of the Saints' defensive coaching staff in presenting these materials to Saints' players in team meetings and in other contexts constitutes persistent and flagrant contempt for clear League rules and policies regarding player safety.

According to Tagliabue, the combination of exhortations ("kill the head and the body will die"), terminology ("cartoff," "knockout"), and the existence of a pay-for-performance program represented the Saints' organizational dereliction of duties in upholding the league's policies on player safety.

This mostly defined the "severe misconduct"[303] to which Tagliabue referred in his ruling; he also included the "indefensible obstruction"[304] by the Saints as part of this misconduct. As Tagliabue put it, the Saints' coaches and other employees "led a deliberate, unprecedented and effective effort to obstruct the NFL's investigation."[305]

In explaining his findings on the Saints, Tagliabue first outlined the history of performance pools in the NFL. This examination provided important context for the events in question, especially in relation to the roles of the Saints' coaches.

Tagliabue asserted -- about the Saints' pay-for-performance program -- that "the evidence before [him] reflect[ed] the realities of NFL team workplaces."[306] He further illustrated that "a culture has evolved -- that has led to acceptance of pay-for-performance reward programs."[307]

Complicating matters further, Tagliabue explained the rules governing (i.e., prohibiting) pay-for-performance programs in the NFL "lack[ed] clarity"[308] and that current league policy was bereft of a "concrete set of guidelines or prohibitions related to performance pools."[309] Tagliabue finished by stating that the NFL's policy was not "fully articulated"[310] in this area.

Equally revealing, Tagliabue said:[311]

> Most important, no matter what the League rules and policies are or have been, if many teams in the League allow pay-for-performance programs to operate in the locker room, as seems to be the case, and, in the main, the League has tolerated this behavior without punishment of players, then many players may not have a clear understanding that such behavior is prohibited or where the lines are between permissible and impermissible conduct.

In other words, the NFL's prior stance on performance pools was mostly tolerant and the policies governing them -- that is, the rules that teams must follow -- were vague and amorphous. No matter, according to Tagliabue, it was the team's responsibility (and not the players) to differentiate between "permissible and impermissible" conduct and lead accordingly.

Tagliabue continued by citing examples of league investigations into pay-for-performance programs in Green Bay ('08) and New England ('07), where the levied discipline was simply a $25,000 team fine. Tagliabue explained:[312]

> ... the League has emphasized club responsibility for ensuring player compliance with League policies, and has disciplined clubs - - but not players - - for non-compliance.
>
> For example, in separate instances involving the Green Bay Packers and New England Patriots in 2007 and 2008, the League fined the clubs $25,000 or less, without disciplining any player.

These examples, precedents for discipline in related cases under Goodell, illustrated Goodell's sharp departure from what Tagliabue earlier called "uniformity of standards for parties similarly situated."[313]

Coupled with these illustrations was Paul Tagliabue's review of a 1997 *ESPN* television segment that featured the Green Bay Packers' "Smash4Cash" program. Tagliabue explained that the NFL exonerated the Packers of any wrongdoing at the time. A report on that program stated:[314]

> What does the NFL have to say about this incentive program that players insist is not a bounty?

A league spokesman said the Smash4Cash program is within the rules as long as players use their own monies; the amounts are not exorbitant; and the payments are not for illegal hits.

This example was almost identical to the Saints' program: player interviews and testimony from Saints' coaches universally corroborated that the Saints' performance program only rewarded legal plays in games the Saints won. The only difference from the aforementioned example was an allegation of one bounty, one that was never proven to be true.

In his cross examination before Paul Tagliabue, Joe Vitt testified that not only did many teams in the NFL operate pay-for-performance programs -- citing examples from Kansas City and Seattle where he previously coached -- but he also relayed that Gregg Williams decided to "stand firm to take the heat" on the league's allegations.

Vitt fully explained:[315]

> I've got a text from Mr. Williams, if we want to see it, that he sent to me back in February, the first time that he was - the second time he was called into the league office; he says to me, 24 teams have reached out to me and asked me to take the hit on this because they all do it.
>
> Do you want to see that, Mr. Commissioner? ... "Yes," Tagliabue said. ...
>
> [Vitt read Williams' text]: "For your information, I've had 20-plus teams reach out to me saying that I must stand firm to take the heat because all teams do this. Fuck me."

The picture that emerged from Tagliabue's historical examination of pay-for-performance systems detailed: 1.) a prevalence of performance pools league-wide; 2.) the NFL's heretofore tolerance of said programs; and 3.) minimal team fines for disciplinary measures.

With this ubiquity of pay-for-performance programs, and with the wrist-slap penalties previously associated with their existence, the Saints perhaps took less than seriously the NFL's investigation.

When the NFL pressed and redoubled their efforts into what Saints' coaches likely viewed as a minor issue, the Saints apparently rebuffed NFL investigators. As Tagliabue noted:[316]

> ... the Saints' coaches here resented the League's investigative / enforcement efforts and improperly resisted and blocked them.

Likely as retribution for the Saints' non-cooperation, in part, Roger Goodell eviscerated the team with sanctions unseen before in NFL history, and inconsistent with their misdeeds. As Paul Tagliabue said, Goodell's actions "represented a severe competitive penalty for the Saints' team, its fans and indirectly for the New Orleans / Gulf Coast region."[317]

Though it seemed clear, through his historical examination, that Tagliabue viewed Goodell's actions as inappropriately severe, he nevertheless blamed Saints' coaches and management for wrongdoing -- for establishing a pay-for-performance system; for engaging in rhetoric and employing terminology inconsistent with the league's policies on player safety; and for failing to cooperate with the NFL's investigation.

For these reasons, he held the Saints' organization responsible for the events of Bountygate.

***

After the release of Tagliabue's ruling, the NFLPA responded:[318]

> We believe that when a fair due process takes place, a fair outcome is the result.
>
> We are pleased that Paul Tagliabue, as the appointed hearings officer, agreed with the NFL Players Association that previously issued discipline was inappropriate in the matter of the alleged New Orleans Saints bounty program.
>
> Vacating all discipline affirms the players' unwavering position that all allegations the League made about their alleged "intent-to-injure" were utterly and completely false.
>
> We are happy for our members.

Roger Goodell, though, wasn't quite as pleased with Tagliabue's result. Goodell, unsurprisingly, reiterated his beliefs and validated his previous actions. He said:[319]

> I was disappointed [Tagliabue] could find conduct detrimental and there is no discipline, that he could excuse that type of

accountability as a coach's responsibility. I don't share that perspective ...

I don't accept that philosophy. To me, everybody is accountable ...

Everyone, that is, except for Roger Goodell.

***

In examining the dual tenets of Tagliabue's ruling -- that the coaches were culpable, but the players were not -- one must accept an explanation that rests upon a tenuous logic.

Specifically, Tagliabue's ruling posited that the Saints' coaches and management were guilty of establishing a program, purportedly interlaced with the urgings of malice, that Saints players never implemented to the detriment of any opponent's wellbeing during the three seasons the Saints supposedly operated this program.

In short, Tagliabue's ruling was a clear reflection that whatever allegedly transpired in the locker room for motivational purposes never morphed into malice on the field.

As Joe Vitt was fond of repeatedly saying:[320]

> I said that under no circumstances have any of our players ever crossed the white line with the intent of injuring, maiming or taking away the career of another player in the National Football League ...
>
> It never happened.

***

With Tagliabue's ruling, Bountygate was all but over and the Saints' nightmarish 2012 season was following suit.

As the regular season was winding down, there was still a bit more history to be made.

22: looming infamy

The Sunday after Paul Tagliabue issued his ruling, the Saints produced one of their best performances of the season in beating the Tampa Bay Buccaneers 41-0 in the Superdome. The Saints' defense posted their first shutout since 1995, temporarily suspending the pending infamy with which they'd eventually be saddled.

Drew Brees regained his form after the particularly vicious three-game stretch that preceded this game. He registered a 124.6 passer rating while throwing for 307 yards and four touchdowns.

The next week in Dallas, the Saints escaped with a 34-31 overtime victory after blowing a fourteen-point fourth quarter lead. The offense posted a season-high 562 yards, and for much of the game, looked like their formerly dominant selves.

The defense, on the other hand, surrendered an atrocious eight yards per play; gave up two 58-yard touchdown receptions to Dez Bryant in the span of eight minutes; and allowed the Cowboys to score two touchdowns within the game's final four minutes to tie the score.

When Garrett Hartley kicked the 20-yard game-winning field goal, the Saints improved to 7-8 with an opportunity to finish the season at .500 in the Superdome against the Carolina Panthers.

Week 17, however, turned out to be perhaps the Saints' worst defensive performance of the season. The Panthers racked up 530 yards -- a season high against the Saints' defense -- and scored 44 points, the second-most points allowed by the Saints during the 2012 season.

In the second half the Panthers scored 31 points against a defense that, perhaps, had quit on its coach. With a 44-38 loss the Saints finished the season at 7-9, equaling their season-worst finish (2007) during the Sean Payton era.

***

When the NFL's 2012 regular season concluded, the Saints stood alone as the first team in NFL history to surrender more than 7,000 yards in a single-season. This eclipsed the previous league-worst mark of 6,793 yards allowed by the 1981 Baltimore Colts.

Further, the Saints' defense surrendered a modern-era worst 6.5 yards per play, exceeding the 2008 (0-16) Detroit Lions' prior all-time worst mark of 6.4 yards allowed per play.

For a team intent on rebuilding its defense under one of the NFL's most-respected defensive minds in Steve Spagnuolo, the Saints' defense flamed out spectacularly in 2012. Grotesquely mirroring a 2011 season where the Saints' offense set the NFL record for yards gained in a season, the 2012 Saints' defense set its own mark for historic futility in surrendering the most yards in a season.

It was a suitable microcosm for the team's sudden reversal of fortune.

***

Ten days after the Panthers beat the Saints to end the regular season, Sean Payton signed a new five-year contract with the Saints.

An *ESPN* report on the contract stated:[321]

> New Orleans Saints coach Sean Payton has signed a five-year contract extension that will run through the 2017 season.
>
> The team announced the extension Wednesday but did not release details. The deal is expected to pay Payton more than $8 million annually, which should establish him as the NFL's highest-paid coach, a league source told ESPN. Payton agreed to the deal in principle on Dec. 29.

With the new contract for Sean Payton, Saints' fans breathed a collective sigh of relief as the team and the fanbase looked to start anew in 2013.

Though Payton was officially in the fold for 2013 and beyond, he still awaited reinstatement from Roger Goodell. This state of purgatory would last a bit longer, and in the meantime, New Orleans prepared to host the Super Bowl.

***

On January 17th, 2013, Judge Ginger Berrigan dismissed Jonathan Vilma's defamation lawsuit against Roger Goodell, effectively ending Bountygate.

Berrigan crystallized her ruling like this:[322]

While the Court is extremely disturbed by the fundamental lack of due process in Goodell's denying the players the identities of and the right to confront their accusers, that was substantially rectified later in the process.

So while the process was initially procedurally flawed, the statements were ultimately found to have enough support to defeat the defamation claims.

With the last of the litigation resolved, Bountygate concluded and was ready to define its legacy.

the legacy of bountygate

legacy: the nfl's motives

As noted early in the book, the NFL opted to make Bountygate a public spectacle.

With Roger Goodell and the NFL in control of publicizing the Bountygate events, why would they choose to make it an issue for public consumption? On its surface, especially considering the initial mischaracterization of the events, Bountygate seemed damning to the league.

At a time when public dialogue about football was irrevocably tied to concussions, long-term health consequences of playing the sport, mushrooming injury litigation, and an ownership aloof to the health concerns of its players and retirees, it was an odd decision for the NFL to make public another issue that seemed to illuminate its dark side.

Combined with 200 concussion lawsuits filed on behalf of 4,000 former players, the purported events of Bountygate in the public domain seemed further contrary to the NFL's interests.

Yet despite all of this, Goodell and the NFL, of their own free will, conducted the Bountygate case in an expressly public manner when they were under no obligation to do so. This was obviously a planned decision, and one aimed at benefiting the league. More specifically, it was a tactic in a larger strategy that aimed to alter the conventional narrative surrounding football, its associated culture of violence, and the NFL's role in ensuring the safety of its workforce.

Coupled with the existing, averse conventional wisdom were the anecdotal cases of men like Pittsburgh Steelers' Hall of Fame center Mike Webster who died in 2002 at the age of 50, destitute and homeless. Webster suffered from a swath of post-career physical and mental ailments, deterioration and dementia so bad that Webster would sometimes shock himself unconscious with a taser in order to sleep.[323]

A University of Pittsburgh psychiatry professor concluded Webster was "totally and permanently disabled" and that Webster suffered from "traumatic or punch-drunk encephalopathy, caused by multiple head blows received while playing center in the NFL."[324]

Though it's likely that the entirety of Webster's maladies weren't solely attributable to his NFL career, nor was his decline exclusively the result of the NFL's negligence in addressing Webster's extreme post-career health concerns, the NFL was nevertheless contributory to Webster's demise.

Moreover, the disturbing public details of Webster's post-NFL life and eventual death were extremely damaging to the NFL in the decade since Webster's passing.

There was also the case of 44 year-old Andre Waters, a popular safety from the Philadelphia Eagles who committed suicide in 2006 after battling depression for years.

With portions of Waters' brain preserved for study, Dr. Bennet Omalu noted that Waters' brain exhibited the signs of Alzheimer's disease and that Waters' brain tissue was consistent with that of an 85year-old man. Omalu is perhaps the world's preeminent neuropathologist, and the man credited with identifying and labeling the condition known as Chronic Traumatic Encephalopathy (CTE), a degenerative brain disease linked to repeated head trauma.

Dr. Omalu ruled that Andre Waters' brain damage was either brought on or exacerbated by multiple concussions from his days in the NFL.[325]

Then there was Dave Duerson, a safety for the legendary 1985 Chicago Bears' defense. A graduate of Notre Dame, a businessman in his post-career life, Duerson committed suicide in 2011 by shooting himself in the chest at the age of 50. In his suicide note, Duerson requested his brain be donated to the NFL's brain bank for study.

Dr. Anne McKee, in association with the Center for the Study of Traumatic Encephalopathy at Boston University's School of Medicine, stated that Duerson "had classic pathology of CTE and no evidence of any other disease and he [had] severe involvement of all the [brain] structures that affect things like judgment, inhibition, impulse control, mood and memory."[326]

More recently Junior Seau, one of the NFL's marquee players in recent years -- a Hall of Famer, a 20-year NFL veteran, and a community leader -- committed suicide by shooting himself in the chest at the age of 43. Seau's family donated Seau's brain for study soon after his death.

The National Institutes of Health ruled in their findings on Seau's brain: "The type of findings seen in Mr. Seau's brain have been recently reported in autopsies of individuals with exposure to repetitive head injury, including professional and amateur athletes who played contact sports, individuals with multiple concussions, and veterans exposed to blast injury and other trauma."[327]

***

With cases like these -- heartbreaking, terrifying, and damaging -- in the public domain shaping perceptions associated with professional football, combined with the prevalence of concussion lawsuits being filed, the NFL was vulnerable.

As the public narrative became overwhelming in its revelation of the health risks involved in playing football, and damning of the NFL's inviolable association with those risks, the NFL's popularity and long-term profitability seemed suddenly threatened.

In an effort, then, to alter the conventional wisdom, to balance a dialogue heavily-weighted against the NFL's interests, Roger Goodell and the NFL proactively undertook a series of initiatives aimed at managing this burgeoning crisis in 2012.

Bountygate was almost certainly just one tactic in their larger strategy, its tactics collectively executed during the 2012 offseason. This was public relations 101: crisis mitigation.

Some of these strategically-timed tactics included:

* **A Case Study on the Life Expectancy of NFL Players**

In May 2012, the NFL released a study from the *National Institute for Occupational Safety and Health* that posited NFL players had a longer life expectancy than that of the general population. This study's conclusion was misleading, and the idea that playing football contributed to a longer, healthier life was silly in its own right.

Regardless of the science backing the study, the limited factors it used in reaching its conclusions, and its failure to account for quality of life among retirees, the study's chief purpose was to establish a perception more favorable to the league.

* **A Mandate on Hip, Knee, and Thigh Pads**

In late May 2012, NFL owners passed a safety mandate requiring NFL players to wear thigh, hip, and knee pads starting in 2013.

This was part of the NFL's "common sense" approach to safety. This, though, came at a time when the NFL didn't require independent neurologists to evaluate players during games; continued to push for an expansion of the regular season; and authorized a full season of Thursday night football, games that prevented adequate recovery time for NFL players.

This mandate seemed to be more about pretense than protection, but the NFL nevertheless touted it as indicative of its dedication to player safety.

* The "Heads Up Football" Initiative

In association with USA Football, football's national governing body, the NFL billed the "Heads Up Football" initiative as "the new standard in player safety."[328]

This August 2012 campaign championed the NFL's commitment to teaching football players -- both youth and professional -- the proper tackling techniques in an effort to promote a safer playing environment.

Unveiled in widespread distribution across television and web platforms just prior to the NFL regular season, this initiative sought to build on the message the NFL had established throughout the earlier months of 2012.

***

These tactics were all aimed, in part at least, at more favorably shaping the perception of the NFL's role in protecting the safety of its players. Bountygate was no different in this regard.

With Bountygate, Roger Goodell and the NFL established a narrative that illustrated the NFL would punish harshly any action compromising the safety of its players.

And though the Saints were never guilty of what Goodell accused them (targeting and injuring opponents for money), that was always of secondary importance to Goodell and the NFL. What was most important was making a clear, loud, public declaration that the health of its players was a top priority. If that meant unjustly dismantling a franchise in the process, if that meant unfairly tarnishing the reputations of the men involved, then so be it.

Bountygate was "Protect the Shield" at its basest.

The facts of the case, and the evidence supporting Goodell's claims, were always of minor consequence to Roger Goodell. Of major consequence was the effective delivery of his message, the shaping of a perception, the shifting of blame away from a culture of violence systemic to and nurtured by the NFL to an isolated set of what Goodell disingenuously labeled as misguided, rogue individuals poisoning the sanctity of the NFL.

It was never about what the Saints did wrong -- which wasn't all that much, or all that different from what occurred in the NFL on a routine basis -- it was only about what the NFL could gain by accusing the Saints of doing so, rightly or wrongly.

Bountygate was about the NFL crafting facades and fortifying moats, of re-engineering a more favorable conventional wisdom, of insulating themselves from the threat of future litigation, of protecting their brand and its profitability at all costs.

In its most naked form, Bountygate wasn't so much about player safety as it was a vehicle for delivering a message beneficial to the league and a maneuver for shifting liability away from its owners.

legacy: roger goodell's credibility

An issue central to Bountygate, during both the saga and its aftermath, was the credibility of Roger Goodell.

As the events of Bountygate unfolded, Roger Goodell exhibited a consistent disregard for accuracy and, in some cases, the truth. As we learned, one of the defining patterns of Bountygate was that of unsubstantiated claims followed by eventual disprovals.

This pattern centered on many individuals and events, including these false claims:

* Scott Fujita's involvement in Bountygate

* Mike Ornstein's email detailing a bounty on Aaron Rodgers

* Mike Ornstein's corroboration of Vilma pledging the alleged Favre bounty

* Joe Vitt's $5,000 pledge towards the alleged Favre bounty

* Jimmy Kennedy's involvement with the alleged Favre bounty

* Anthony Hargrove demanding payment ("pay me my money") for the alleged Favre bounty

* Anthony Hargrove's admission of a bounty program

* Mike Cerullo collecting "two five stacks"

* Mike Cerullo's accurate transcription of the "handwritten note"

* Three paid "cart-offs" occurring during the Saints-Bills 2009 game

* Three paid "cart-offs" occurring during a Saints-Panthers 2009 game

* The Saints pledging bounties on Kurt Warner, Aaron Rodgers, and Cam Newton

Though these claims established a perception of malice and guilt, they all ultimately proved baseless.

As opposed to incidentally misrepresenting an isolated claim, Goodell provided a consistent, steady stream of flawed accusations that undermined both his Bountygate claims and his credibility as a whole. The larger problem was that Bountygate mirrored the 2008 Spygate scandal in many aspects.

More than anything, the combined events of Bountygate and Spygate revealed Goodell's penchant for mishandling evidence and obscuring the truth.

The Spygate saga, in short, centered on allegations that the New England Patriots illegally videotaped their opponents' defensive signals (and some practice sessions) from 2000 - 2007. In levying sanctions for these purported misdeeds, Roger Goodell issued fines of $500,000 and $250,000 to Bill Belichick and the New England Patriots, respectively. Goodell also withheld a first-round draft pick from the team.

After completing his investigation and issuing punishments, Goodell destroyed all of the Spygate evidence. For this act, Roger Goodell was called before Senator Arlen Specter to explain his actions. A February 2008 *ESPN* report explained:[329]

> Bill Belichick has been illegally taping opponents' defensive signals since he became the New England Patriots' coach in 2000, according to Sen. Arlen Specter, who said NFL commissioner Roger Goodell told him that during a meeting Wednesday ...
>
> Specter said Goodell gave him that information during the 1-hour, 40-minute meeting, which was requested by Specter so the commissioner could explain his reasons for destroying the Spygate tapes and notes.

These "tapes" were the actual video footage captured by the Patriots, revealing what they taped and against who they schemed. After reviewing the tapes, Goodell destroyed them. The reasons for this are unclear, and under questioning, Goodell simply said he thought "it was the right thing to do."[330]

When pressed by Specter to explain himself further, Goodell claimed he destroyed the evidence in order to prevent other teams from accessing the footage. Of this nonsensical explanation, *ESPN* reported:[331]

> [Specter] scoffed at the reasons Goodell gave for destroying the tapes and notes, particularly about trying to keep them out of

> competitors' hands and because Belichick had admitted to the taping.
>
> "What's that got to do with it? There's an admission of guilt, you preserve the evidence," Specter said. As for keeping the tapes out of the hands of others: "All you have to do is lock up the tapes."

The same *ESPN* report further noted:[332]

> Specter wants to know why penalties were imposed on Belichick before the full extent of the wrongdoing was known and the tapes destroyed in a two-week span.
>
> Asked if he thinks there was a coverup, Specter demurred. "There was an enormous amount of haste," Specter said.

In Spygate, it became impossible to separate facts from allegations. Goodell's destruction of evidence allowed him to make claims without supporting them; shroud the full, true extent of the misdeed; and control the outcome of the scandal to his liking.

Bountygate almost directly mirrored this pattern of haphazard evidentiary standards, opacity, and a premature imposition of discipline. As the *ESPN* article on Spygate noted, Senator Specter "questioned the quality of the NFL's investigation" as a whole.[333]

In total, the Bountygate investigation resulted in the bizarrely abrupt departure of its chief investigator midway through the events; a much smaller body of "evidence" than originally claimed; the many disprovals of unsubstantiated allegations; the utilization of a principal witness (Mike Cerullo) with a history of mendacity and apparent ulterior motive; and the ultimate voiding of all discipline levied on the accused players.

These were clear indications of a poorly-executed process, and Roger Goodell's credibility was directly tied to this. Not only was it evident that Goodell mishandled the Bountygate investigation, he had a history of engaging in similar activity.

For two of the NFL's biggest "scandals" during Goodell's reign to be conducted so poorly and opaquely was a reflection of Goodell's ability and/or desire to conduct an open, fair process.

***

In the months following the public disclosure of Bountygate, Roger Goodell found himself repeatedly admonished by NFL players. As one of the primary leaders of the NFLPA, Drew Brees was the harshest of Goodell's critics.

In July of 2012, Brees said of Roger Goodell:[334]

> Nobody trusts him. I'm not talking about a DUI, or using a gun in a strip club, which are pretty clear violations. I think there're too many times where the league has come to its decision in a case before calling a guy in, and the interview is just a façade.
>
> I think now if a guy has to come in to talk to Roger, he'll be very hesitant because he'll think the conclusion has already been reached.

By December, Brees' comments were much more succinct when he said "the league office and commissioner Goodell have very little to no credibility with us as players." [335]

During this timeframe, Drew Brees wasn't the only player to levy criticism on Goodell. In May of 2012, Jay Feely (the Arizona Cardinals' NFLPA representative) said of Goodell: "There's a general distrust for him."[336]

Feely expanded on this notion:[337]

> A lot of players don't believe [Goodell] has their best interests at heart. If he did, he wouldn't have 200-plus workmen's compensation complaints caught up in the appeals process. He wouldn't be dismissing disability claims right off the bat. There are so many things that happen behind the scenes that fans don't know about that make players distrust him.

A January 2013 poll conducted by *USA Today* revealed that 61% of NFL players disapproved of Goodell's performance as commissioner:[338]

> In a recent poll of NFL players conducted by USA TODAY Sports, 61% said they disapprove of the job Goodell has done overall, with most focusing on the increased fines of players for dangerous hits on defenseless receivers and quarterbacks and the perception of the commissioner's investigation into the bounty matter.

This disapproval rating arose out of the players' skepticism for Goodell's true motivations, and the extreme manner in which he disciplined them during his reign.

Much of this rancor and distrust, too, traced back to 2010 prior to the league's lockout of the players. During the lead-up to the lockout, Goodell proactively attempted to assuage player concerns in meetings with several teams. While positioning himself as neutral, Goodell sought to minimize fears he was simply a mouthpiece for the owners' demands. These meetings, though, did not go so well for Goodell.

NFLPA Executive Director De Smith explained:[339]

> What offended [the players] is that [Goodell] told them he was neutral and he actually thought they'd believe it. That was the beginning -- it has led us to a lack of credibility from the players to Roger, and the NFL.

This episode, followed by the owners' lockout of the players, underpinned the players' distrust of Goodell and initiated the gradual erosion of his credibility.

More recently, Goodell has been prone to frame many of his initiatives under the guise of "player safety." While this sounds sensible and righteous on the surface, Goodell's underlying motivations have been much less clear.

Pittsburgh Steelers' linebacker James Harrison explained:[340]

> I feel like what he's doing is not totally for the safety of players. ... A lot of stuff they've done, (such as) fining guys crazy amounts of money for helmet-to-helmet hits and all that and saying you're doing this for the safety of players. But yet you want to add extra games to the regular season.
>
> In the true interest of player safety, I would have no issue with it. But that's not what it's about. It's about money.

Whether Harrison is correct or not about Goodell's actions being "about money," it's nevertheless a reflection of a continuing sentiment that casts doubt on the authenticity of Roger Goodell's actions. With Bountygate, many of Goodell's claims were inauthentic and his process was starkly unfair as he repeatedly denied the accused access to evidence and witnesses claiming to damn them.

Bountygate served to further cement the notion that Goodell, granted with sweeping powers, lacked the judgment to properly wield that authority. Were Goodell's Bountygate actions beyond reproach, it's unlikely Goodell would have: 1.) had his originally-levied player discipline unanimously overturned by a three-person appeals' panel; 2.) faced sharp criticism from a federal judge for his actions; and 3.) had his amended player sanctions voided in full by his former boss.

That damning sequence clearly illustrated a lack of credible action from Goodell during Bountygate; created a pattern of slipshod (or cynical) investigational machinations in light of Spygate; and exacerbated the concerns of NFL players who distrusted Roger Goodell.

Goodell's credibility, unwittingly, was among the many casualties of Bountygate.

legacy: why the saints?

The extreme sanctions dispensed by Roger Goodell during Bountygate were the result of a confluence of events: a choice to alter a culture's established norms; an attempt to protect an entity from the threat of class litigation; and one man's desire to harshly punish a franchise he viewed as intransigent, and outside the bounds of his governing thumb.

This is the theory to which I subscribe.

The Saints, without question, were guilty of violating league rules. They operated a pay-for-performance program that rewarded legal plays in games the Saints won. This is technically an Article 14 violation of the league's collective bargaining agreement, an act that awarded non-contract bonuses that violate salary cap provisions.

What the Saints were not guilty of, however, was the targeting and injuring of opponents for petty cash.

The Saints' relatively benign violation -- one Paul Tagliabue admitted was endemic to the NFL and heretofore tolerated by the league -- added to (what I believe was) Roger Goodell's rooted perception of a franchise that operated in a manner he deemed unsuitable. Prior to Bountygate, the Payton-era Saints were not without their black marks.

Under Payton, the Saints had run afoul of the league's media policy; associated themselves with a convicted felon in Mike Ornstein; and garnered regrettable headlines during an episode involving the theft of prescription drugs on the team's premises.

During his time as Saints' coach, Sean Payton sometimes disregarded the NFL's media policies: banning reporters from access to the team and showing up late to press conferences, among other things. These missteps culminated during Super Bowl week in 2010 when the Saints arrived an hour late for media day. As a linchpin of the NFL's calendar of events in the weekly lead-up to the Super Bowl, media day attracts thousands of legitimate media from around the globe to interview the participating teams. The NFL places a high enough priority on this event that it's televised live.

At the time, *ESPN's* Pat Yasinskas reported "league officials were freaking out"[341] when the Saints delayed media day by an hour. While

Sean Payton later explained that the team's delay was due to several players oversleeping and failing to arrive to the team bus on time, this event nonetheless infuriated the NFL.

Sean Payton then compounded this mistake by showing up to the post-Super Bowl press conference hungover. To this Payton admitted in his book, *Home Team: Coaching the Saints and New Orleans Back to Life*.[342]

> Did I mention the press conference was scheduled for 8:30 a.m.? ... I'd been asleep and hour and 40 minutes, and I'd had a couple cocktails and some Amstel Light. OK, more than a couple. ...
>
> What can I say? I'm lucky I could string a sentence together at all. I got back in the Town Car and fell asleep on the ride back to the hotel. The next thing I remember, I was on the team charter flying home. That was Monday. It's all a bit of a blur. Have you ever seen the movie, "The Hangover," where the guy is asking, "How did this lion get here? Where did my tooth go? Isn't that Mike Tyson? That was Monday for me.

Though Payton's actions the day after the Super Bowl were both good-natured and harmless, they almost certainly alienated the straight-laced Roger Goodell.

***

In addition to this, the Saints' association with Mike Ornstein likely added to Goodell's perception of the Saints-as-rogue. As detailed earlier Ornstein was a twice-convicted felon, once guilty of attempting to defraud the NFL of $350,000.

Ornstein also presided over the marketing management of Reggie Bush while Bush was in college, Ornstein's role ultimately resulting in the surrendering of Bush's Heisman trophy among other things.

Though Ornstein was never a Saints' employee -- only an associate and periodic consultant under the Payton-era Saints -- his attachment to the team in light of his past deeds likely did the Saints no favors, at least in regard to Goodell's perception of the franchise.

***

This all paled in comparison to the Vicodin scandal that went public in May of 2010. In that scandal, the Saints then-Security Director, Geoff Santini, accused Joe Vitt of stealing Vicodin from the team's drug supply and sharing it with Sean Payton. Santini also accused Saints' General Manager Mickey Loomis of covering up the alleged theft in order to protect Payton.

For these accusations, Santini sued the Saints.

According to Santini's lawsuit against the Saints, Vitt -- who had a legal prescription for Vicodin due to a "painful medical condition"[343] -- stole 110 pills during a four-month period (about one pill a day, in other words) in 2009. He allegedly shared them with Payton during this time.

When this scandal went public, the Saints released a statement that read:[344]

> A former employee who resigned just before the 2009 regular season threatened to go public with these unfounded charges unless we agreed to pay him an exorbitant sum of money. We refused and now he has gone public.
>
> We will aggressively defend these false allegations in court. We will not have any further comment on this matter at this time. Rather we look forward to welcoming our rookie players and want our focus to be on continuing our preparations for the 2010 Football Season and defending our title.

Mike Florio of *Pro Football Talk* reported that the "exorbitant sum" demanded by Santini was $2 million.[345]

Soon after the allegations, Sean Payton responded:[346]

> I have reviewed Geoff Santini's lawsuit and the unwarranted publicity it has received. I have never abused or stolen Vicodin or any other medication and I fully support the Saints' position in this matter as expressed by Greg Bensel yesterday.

Eventually, Santini withdrew his lawsuit after the Saints invoked a clause in Santini's contract that allowed them to settle the dispute via arbitration instead of civil litigation.

This maneuver prevented either party (the Saints or Santini) from speaking publicly about the case.

The DEA separately launched an investigation into the alleged theft, a potential federal crime for the team's lack of organizational oversight.[347]

As of September 2012, the DEA investigation was ongoing. From the start, the NFL has refrained from commenting on this case.

***

This event temporarily maligned the Saints and its allegations -- whether true or not -- must have angered Roger Goodell.

Combined with all of these preceding events were the allegations of the bounty on Brett Favre. The NFL first learned of this alleged bounty during the 2010 offseason after Brad Childress complained to the league. This accusation added to, in all likelihood, Goodell's presumption that the Saints believed they were above his law.

For a commissioner defined by his iron-fisted ways, Roger Goodell almost certainly decided to intercede and "right" what he perceived to be wrong in New Orleans.

He did this partly by initiating the bounty investigation, one he claimed the Saints obstructed over the course of two seasons. For this final straw of defiance, Goodell eviscerated the Saints based on a flimsy and faulty set of allegations, all under the benevolent guise of "player safety."

Concurrently, this enabled Goodell to both publicly establish a "culture change" narrative and further build a protective measure against concussion litigation.

It was theoretically a win on multiple fronts for Goodell.

The Saints, as his culture-changing scapegoat, were nonetheless worthy of punishment -- in his eyes -- for an accumulation of misdeeds and allegations he deemed unacceptable. Instead of quietly punishing the team and moving forward, Goodell decided to opportunistically seize the moment and craft a multilayered benefit for the NFL when the time was right. That time was the 2012 offseason.

Collateral damage be damned.

legacy: a final word

As for Bountygate, in the end, it's clear what happened.

Roger Goodell took one alleged, unproven bounty from seasons ago and distorted it to represent a three-year pay-to-injure program; decimated the Saints with sanctions; held them high as a trophy of culture change; and conducted a highly-visible media campaign under the auspices of protecting the safety of the NFL's workforce.

Peripherally, Roger Goodell devastated a franchise that dared defy his dictates, while simultaneously exacting retribution on a group of NFL management (Payton, Williams, Vitt, Loomis) he was unable to keep under his rule of law for years.

The facts of the Bountygate case and the evidence underpinning its end result -- flaccid, illusory, and unreliable -- never mattered to the man whose intent was both punitive and self-serving.

A March 2013 *ESPN* report on Roger Goodell by Pulitzer-prize winner Don Van Natta, Jr. relayed this distillation of the Bountygate investigation:[348]

> ESPN has exclusively obtained Bountygate documents including confidential transcripts of the private four-day appeal hearing held by former commissioner Tagliabue late last year.
>
> The documents show an investigation remarkable for its limited scope -- only one Saints player spoke to investigators, for example -- and for damning accusations that league officials quietly retracted in later memos or chose not to introduce as evidence.

A year after the initial accusations, after the scandal's conclusion, and after the damage done, the truth finally started to emerge.

Among the facts of Bountygate are these:

* Many of the NFL's accusations and intimations were ultimately unsubstantiated and untrue.

* The NFL failed to discipline Saints' players for any on-field misconduct as a result of the league's Bountygate allegations.

* The Saints injured fewer players than all but one team during the timeframe Goodell accused them of operating an injury program. Contrasted to their characterization as malicious, the Saints' defense in fact was one of the NFL's most passive and non-threatening.

* Joe Vitt, Jonathan Vilma, and six other current and former Saints' players testified under oath in federal court that Vilma, nor anyone else, pledged a bounty on Brett Favre. The NFL, on the other hand, produced no witness who testified under oath in court that a bounty in fact existed.

* Paul Tagliabue, after reviewing the entirety of the evidence and presiding over the witness testimony of every key figure, still failed to establish the legitimacy of the alleged Favre bounty.

* A three-person panel consisting of two retired judges and one law professor unanimously ruled that Roger Goodell violated the collective bargaining agreement.

* A federal judge repeatedly criticized Goodell's actions for their "fundamental lack of due process."

* Paul Tagliabue permanently voided the discipline levied on the accused players, and further refused to issue any amended sanctions whatsoever.

***

Early in 2013, NFLPA Executive Director DeMaurice Smith appeared on *ESPN* to talk about Bountygate.

He ended with this fitting, final commentary:[349]

> Now frankly I will tell you, do I think the fans in New Orleans got the raw end of that deal? Yes they did.
>
> Do I know that Sean Payton got the raw end of that deal?
>
> Yes he did, because I know from reading each and every page of that transcript that what the National Football League said occurred never occurred.

coda: sean payton, a second act

On Tuesday January 22nd, 2013, Roger Goodell reinstated Sean Payton as the Saints' head coach.

Two days later Payton fired defensive coordinator Steve Spagnuolo, signaling the team's forward-looking mission heading into 2013. Days prior Aaron Kromer, the Saints' offensive line coach and 2012 interim-interim head coach, departed for the Chicago Bears. Absent Spagnuolo and Kromer, two faces of the team's 2012 lackluster performance, Sean Payton set out to again rebuild the Saints' franchise into a championship contender.

In early February of 2013, Payton hired the brash, colorful Rob Ryan to lead the Saints' defense.

For the third time in five years, Sean Payton aimed to reengineer his defense in the face of its shortcomings. Similarly, the symbolism of this move mirrored the Saints' organizational need to refortify its own defenses in the aftermath of Bountygate.

In hiring the controversial and outspoken Ryan, Sean Payton revealed that his temerity and his verve -- the same attributes that culminated in "Ambush," the Super Bowl 44-altering onsides kick -- were still intact and unbowed.

Once crumbled in the wake of Hurricane Katrina, now reeling from the scuds of Bountygate, the Saints seek yet another rebirth under the leadership of Sean Payton and Mickey Loomis.

A second act is underway.

At once down, but never out.

###

about the author

* Reid Gilbert is a freelance writer and Saints' fanatic. You can learn more at reidgilbert.com.

* Follow Reid on Twitter @ReidG75.

* Connect to Reid's Saints' blog at saintswin.com.

book acknowledgements

* To Caroline, for her tolerance, support, love, and good humor

* To all my friends in the "Illegitimate Media," a fitting label coined by the inimitable Grandmaster Wang at moosedenied

* To Jeffrey at the Library Chronicles, for suggesting that I undertake this effort

* To Mike Florio, for his dogged and objective analysis of Bountygate that proved essential to understanding the scandal's dynamics in granular detail

* To Stephanie Stradley and SaintsReport, for their archives of Bountygate's many legal filings

* To all those crazy bastards in :bigbow: The Zoo

* To the accused parties, especially Jonathan Vilma and Joe Vitt, for fighting back

* Book cover art by Bellina Creative Design (www.bellinacreative.com)

end notes

Chapter 1

1. Pro Football Reference: http://www.pro-football-reference.com/coaches/WillGr0.htm

2. The 2003 Bills ranked second in yards allowed, and fifth in points allowed. *PFR*

3. The Redskins' defense improved from 25th in yards allowed and 24th in points allowed to 3rd and 5th in those respective categories in their first season under Williams in 2004. *PFR*

4. Gleaned from an ESPN/Mortensen report on GW's future in Jacksonville : http://www.aolnews.com/2008/12/14/jaguars-could-jettison-gregg-williams-after-just-one-season/

5. GW-JAX-del Rio playcalling: http://jacksonville.com/sports/football/jaguars/2012-03-05/story/ex-jaguars-hayward-and-ingram-no-bounty-under-williams

6. http://blog.nola.com/saintsbeat/2009/01/gregg_williams_interest_in_new.html

7. http://profootballtalk.nbcsports.com/2009/01/18/payton-coughed-up-some-cash-to-get-williams/

8. http://profootballtalk.nbcsports.com/2010/02/08/payton-reflects-on-decision-to-give-up-250000-for-williams/

9. http://www.jonvilma.com/commerce/inthenews/inthenews.asp?reqdate=2/2/2010&id_passed=315

10. In 2010, the Saints ranked 4th in yards allowed and 7th in points allowed. *PFR*

11. http://www.nfl.com/news/story/09000d5d82821ba1/article/williams-independentcontractor-status-fueled-rogue-mentality

12. http://espn.go.com/blog/nflnation/post/_/id/52322/report-gregg-williams-leaving-saints

13. http://profootballtalk.nbcsports.com/2012/01/17/payton-gregg-williams-made-decision-to-leave/

14. http://sports.yahoo.com/news/nfl--saints--defensive-policy-shift-started-with-essential-firing-of-gregg-williams-after-playoff-disaster-vs--49ers.html

15. http://profootballtalk.nbcsports.com/2012/03/21/the-nfls-official-announcement-regarding-bounty-discipline/

16. http://www.bleedinggreennation.com/2009/6/25/924198/a-look-at-past-jim-johnson-proteges

17. http://sportsillustrated.cnn.com/2012/writers/peter_king/01/23/super.bowl.xlvi.matchup/3.html

Chapter 2

18. Mike Florio, Bill Simmons, Mike Tanier, and Dan Le Batard deserve plaudits for their fair reporting on Bountygate, especially Florio whose exhaustive documentation and analysis was essential to understanding the events.

19. http://www.nola.com/saints/index.ssf/2012/03/full_nfl_statement_into_bounty.html

20. http://www.nola.com/saints/index.ssf/2012/03/full_nfl_statement_into_bounty.html

21. http://www.nola.com/saints/index.ssf/2012/03/full_nfl_statement_into_bounty.html

22. http://saintsreport.com/forums/f2/miami-herald-article-goodell-cares-more-cash-228015/#.UOyGbeTO2Po

Chapter 3

23. https://twitter.com/SI_JimTrotter/status/278586087369220096

24. http://www.nola.com/saints/index.ssf/2012/03/in_bounty_scandal_new_orleans.html

25. http://espn.go.com/nfl/story/_/id/7645118/saints-coach-sean-payton-gm-mickey-loomis-deserve-fired-bounty-program

26. http://www.cbssports.com/nfl/story/17546590/saints-vile-bounties-lay-big-hit-on-players-cries-about-goodell-safety

27. http://www.cbssports.com/nfl/story/17546706/saints-team-officials-involved-in-bounty-program-should-pay-dearly

28. http://sportsillustrated.cnn.com/vault/article/magazine/MAG1195695/index.htm

29. http://profootballtalk.nbcsports.com/2012/03/02/gregg-williams-apologizes-for-terrible-mistake/

30. http://www.nola.com/saints/index.ssf/2012/03/new_orleans_saints_staffer_no.html

31. http://www.nola.com/saints/index.ssf/2012/03/new_orleans_saints_staffer_no.html

Chapter 4

32. http://www.nfl.com/news/story/09000d5d827c15b2/article/nfl-announces-management-discipline-in-saints-bounty-matter

33. http://usatoday30.usatoday.com/sports/nfl/Tagliabue-decision-bounty-appeal.pdf (pg 22)

34. http://www.latimes.com/news/opinion/commentary/la-oe-hassett-saints-bounty-program-20120715,0,1284132.story

35. http://sportsillustrated.cnn.com/vault/article/magazine/MAG1195695/2/index.htm

36. http://profootballtalk.nbcsports.com/2012/03/21/gregg-williams-apologizes-again-for-his-role-in-saints-bounty-program/

37. http://www.nola.com/saints/index.ssf/2012/03/saints_coach_sean_payton_speak.html

38. http://www.nfl.com/news/story/09000d5d827c15b2/article/nfl-announces-management-discipline-in-saints-bounty-matter

Chapter 5

39. http://www.pro-football-reference.com/players/B/BreeDr00.htm

40. http://profootballtalk.nbcsports.com/2012/03/03/saints-place-exclusive-franchise-tag-on-drew-brees/

41. In 2008 Brees threw for 5,069 yards, finishing fifteen yards shy of Dan Marino's record-setting 1984 season when he threw for 5,084 yards. Three seasons later Brees would shatter the record, throwing for 5,476 yards.

42. http://sports.espn.go.com/nfl/news/story?id=4884358

Chapter 6

43. http://profootballtalk.nbcsports.com/2012/01/16/carmichael-will-interview-with-raiders/

44. http://www.nola.com/saints/index.ssf/2012/01/st_louis_rams_will_interview_n.html

45. http://usatoday30.usatoday.com/sports/football/nfl/rams/2005-10-10-martz-out_x.htm

46. http://espn.go.com/nfl/story/_/id/7749076/bill-parcells-says-hypocrite-ignore-new-orleans-saints

47. http://www.nfl.com/news/story/09000d5d827f9c4b/article/saints-would-benefit-greatly-from-season-with-bill-parcells

48. http://www.cbssports.com/nfl/story/18325368

49. http://www.cbssports.com/columns/story/17947266/goodell-nfl-hammer-ringleader-payton-and-theyre-right-on-target

Chapter 7

50. http://sports.yahoo.com/nfl/news?slug=ms-silver_gregg_williams_speech_saints_49ers_bounty_040412

51. http://www.nola.com/saints/index.ssf/2012/06/filmmaker_sean_pamphilon_defen.html

52. http://profootballtalk.nbcsports.com/2012/07/13/chiefs-preached-kill-the-head-and-the-body-will-die-too/

53. http://sports.yahoo.com/nfl/news?slug=ms-silver_gregg_williams_speech_saints_49ers_bounty_040412

54. http://www.profootballweekly.com/story/permalink/30795

55. http://usatoday30.usatoday.com/sports/nfl/Tagliabue-decision-bounty-appeal.pdf (pg 21)

56. http://profootballtalk.nbcsports.com/2012/04/10/bill-parcells-will-not-coach-saints/

Chapter 8

57. http://www.nfl.com/news/story/09000d5d828442a0/article/joe-vitt-will-take-over-as-saints-interim-coach-monday

58. http://usatoday30.usatoday.com/sports/basketball/nba/story/2012-04-13/Saints-owner-Benson-buys-NBAs-Hornets/54255918/1

59. http://sports.espn.go.com/nba/news/story?id=5157613

60. http://www.nola.com/hornets/index.ssf/2010/12/nba_makes_its_official_league.html

61. http://espn.go.com/espn/otl/story/_/id/7846290/new-orleans-saints-mickey-loomis-eavesdrop-opposing-coaches-home-games

62. http://profootballtalk.nbcsports.com/2012/04/24/saints-audio-engineer-disputes-eavesdropping-claim/

63. http://profootballtalk.nbcsports.com/2012/04/23/saints-officials-go-on-record-to-dispute-espionage-allegations/

64. http://profootballtalk.nbcsports.com/2012/04/23/saints-officials-go-on-record-to-dispute-espionage-allegations/

Chapter 9

65. http://profootballtalk.nbcsports.com/2012/04/23/saints-officials-go-on-record-to-dispute-espionage-allegations/

66. http://usatoday30.usatoday.com/sports/football/nfl/saints/story/2012-04-26/mickey-loomis-wiretapping-draft/54568310/1

67. http://profootballtalk.nbcsports.com/2012/04/23/saints-call-espn-report-of-loomis-espionage-1000-percent-false/

68. http://espn.go.com/nfl/story/_/id/8265635/state-police-no-evidence-new-orleans-saints-eavesdropping

69. http://profootballtalk.nbcsports.com/2012/04/30/head-of-saints-bounty-probe-submits-resignation-letter/

70. http://profootballtalk.nbcsports.com/2012/04/30/league-says-hummels-departure-has-no-bearing-on-saints-investigation/

71. http://www.nfl.com/news/story/09000d5d828057aa/article/nflpa-hires-outside-counsel-for-players-in-saints-bounty-case

72. http://www.reuters.com/article/2012/04/02/us-nfl-bounty-idUSBRE83110S20120402

73. https://www.nflplayers.com/Articles/Press-Releases/NFLPA-Statement-on-Williams-Audio/

74. https://twitter.com/AlbertBreer/status/191977469417492481

75. http://www.nola.com/saints/index.ssf/2012/04/nfl_commissioner_roger_goodell_21.html

76. http://espn.go.com/nfl/story/_/id/7882067/nfl-statement-text-new-orleans-saints-bounty-penalties

77. http://espn.go.com/nfl/story/_/id/7993744/roger-goodell-confident-bounties-no-longer-issue-nfl-new-orleans-saints-penalties

78. https://www.nflplayers.com/Articles/Player-News/Statement-on-Alleged-Pay-to-Injure-Program-Punishments/

79. http://www.nola.com/saints/index.ssf/2012/05/new_orleans_saints_linebacker_29.html

80. http://www.nola.com/saints/index.ssf/2012/05/new_orleans_saints_de_will_smi_8.html

81. http://www.nola.com/saints/index.ssf/2012/05/nfl_conference_call_with_attor.html

82. http://www.nola.com/saints/index.ssf/2012/05/nfl_conference_call_with_attor.html

83. http://profootballtalk.nbcsports.com/2012/05/03/nfls-outside-lawyer-calls-evidence-against-saints-players-quite-strong/

Chapter 10

84. http://www.nola.com/saints/index.ssf/2012/05/lawyer_for_jonathan_vilma_says.html

85. http://proplayerinsiders.com/nflpa-takes-legal-action-challenges-goodells-authority-over-saints-players/

86. http://proplayerinsiders.com/nflpa-takes-legal-action-challenges-goodells-authority-over-saints-players/

87: http://profootballtalk.nbcsports.com/2012/05/17/vilma-sues-goodell-for-defamation/

88. http://espn.go.com/nfl/story/_/id/7985408/nflpa-seeking-clarity-drew-brees-franchise-tag-status-sources-say

Chapter 11

89. http://profootballtalk.nbcsports.com/2012/03/14/drew-brees-doesnt-sound-willing-to-sign-the-franchise-tender/

90. http://sports.yahoo.com/news/arbitrator-rules-brees-franchise-tag-155328345--nfl.html

91. http://sports.yahoo.com/news/arbitrator-rules-brees-franchise-tag-155328345--nfl.html

92. http://espn.go.com/nfl/story/_/id/8163701/sources-drew-brees-new-orleans-saints-agree-record-contract

93. http://espn.go.com/nfl/story/_/id/7882067/nfl-statement-text-new-orleans-saints-bounty-penalties

94. http://www.nola.com/saints/index.ssf/2012/05/nfl_conference_call_with_attor.html

95. http://sports.yahoo.com/news/nfl--anthony-hargrove-s-declaration-to-nfl-regarding-saints-bounty-scandal.html

96. http://espn.go.com/nfl/story/_/id/7911396/former-new-orleans-saint-anthony-hargrove-disappointed-bounty-declaration-was-leaked

97. http://sportsillustrated.cnn.com/vault/article/magazine/MAG1195695/1/index.htm

98. http://espn.go.com/blog/nfcnorth/post/_/id/43046/anthony-hargrove-alleges-major-nfl-error

99. http://espn.go.com/nfl/story/_/id/7882067/nfl-statement-text-new-orleans-saints-bounty-penalties

100. http://nfllabor.files.wordpress.com/2012/10/10092012-memo-to-clubs.pdf

101. http://espn.go.com/blog/nflnation/post/_/id/65343/jimmy-kennedy-bounty-claims-an-utter-lie

102. http://profootballtalk.nbcsports.com/2012/10/10/league-outs-jimmy-kennedy-as-2010-whistleblower-kennedy-denies-it/

103. http://espn.go.com/nfl/story/_/id/7882067/nfl-statement-text-new-orleans-saints-bounty-penalties

104. http://usatoday30.usatoday.com/sports/nfl/Tagliabue-decision-bounty-appeal.pdf (pg 13)

105. http://usatoday30.usatoday.com/sports/nfl/Tagliabue-decision-bounty-appeal.pdf (pg 13)

106. http://www.nola.com/saints/index.ssf/2011/07/new_orleans_saints_defensive_l_6.html

107. http://www.nola.com/saints/index.ssf/2010/10/marketing_agent_mike_ornstein_1.html

108. http://blog.cleveland.com/metro/2010/11/former_nfl_marketing_vp_setnen.html

109. http://deadspin.com/5890499/meet-the-convicted-felon-who-defrauded-the-nfl-made-reggie-bush-ineligible-and-funded-the-saints-bounty-program

110. http://mike-freeman.blogs.cbssports.com/mcc/blogs/entry/6264363/35066335/2

111. http://www.nfl.com/news/story/09000d5d827c15b2/article/nfl-announces-management-discipline-in-saints-bounty-matter

112. http://espn.go.com/nfl/boxscore?gameId=310908009

113. http://sportsillustrated.cnn.com/2012/football/nfl/05/10/bounty.context.ap/index.html?sct=nfl_t2_a4

114. http://sportsillustrated.cnn.com/2012/football/nfl/05/10/bounty.context.ap/index.html?sct=nfl_t2_a4

115. http://profootballtalk.nbcsports.com/2012/05/10/league-union-at-odds-over-ornstein-email/

116. http://espn.go.com/nfl/story/_/id/8065820/appeal-new-orleans-saints-bounty-suspensions-claim-email-was-joke-sources-say

117. http://profootballtalk.nbcsports.com/2012/05/10/league-union-at-odds-over-ornstein-email/

118. http://profootballtalk.nbcsports.com/2012/05/10/league-union-at-odds-over-ornstein-email/

119. http://sports.yahoo.com/news/nfl--sources--new-orleans-saints-kept-a--ledger--detailing-weekly-earnings-in-bounty-scandal.html

120. http://profootballtalk.nbcsports.com/2012/06/01/ledger-entries-for-bills-game-raise-new-questions-about-saints-bounty-program/

121. http://espn.go.com/nfl/playbyplay?gameId=291108018&period=0

122. http://theangrywhodat.com/2012/06/02/ledger-gate-ok-lets-look-at-the-carolina-game/

123. http://profootballtalk.nbcsports.com/2012/06/02/league-should-simply-release-the-ledger/

124. http://nfllabor.files.wordpress.com/2012/10/10092012-memo-to-clubs.pdf

125. http://nfllabor.files.wordpress.com/2012/10/10092012-memo-to-clubs.pdf

126. http://espn.go.com/nfl/playbyplay?gameId=301107029&period=0

127. https://twitter.com/SI_PeterKing/statuses/214831479946088449

128. http://espn.go.com/nfl/playbyplay?gameId=291018018&period=0

129. http://www.nfl.com/news/story/09000d5d827c15b2/article/nfl-announces-management-discipline-in-saints-bounty-matter

130. http://profootballtalk.nbcsports.com/2013/01/27/payton-explains-ducks-in-a-row-comment/

131. http://espn.go.com/nfl/story/_/id/7882067/nfl-statement-text-new-orleans-saints-bounty-penalties

132. http://espn.go.com/blog/nfcnorth/post/_/id/42996/nfl-bounty-on-favre-at-least-35000

133. http://www.scribd.com/doc/98869069/Vilma-v-Nfl-Complaint (ex. 10, #118)

134. http://www.scribd.com/doc/98869069/Vilma-v-Nfl-Complaint (ex. 10, #121)

135. http://www.nfl.com/news/story/09000d5d829fe235/article/joe-vitt-denies-pledging-money-to-bounty-program

136. http://profootballtalk.nbcsports.com/2012/06/20/league-confirms-vitt-wasnt-accused-of-contributing-to-bounty-pool/

137. http://profootballtalk.nbcsports.com/2012/06/19/nfl-says-williams-ornstein-unnamed-coach-corroborated-vilmas-offer-on-favre/

138. http://profootballtalk.nbcsports.com/2012/06/19/ornstein-denies-telling-nfl-that-vilma-offered-money/

139. http://profootballtalk.nbcsports.com/2012/06/19/ornstein-denies-telling-nfl-that-vilma-offered-money/

140. http://espn.go.com/nfl/story/_/id/8202975/new-orleans-saints-linebacker-jonathan-vilma-testifies

141. http://usatoday30.usatoday.com/sports/nfl/Tagliabue-decision-bounty-appeal.pdf (pg 19)

Chapter 12

142. http://usatoday30.usatoday.com/sports/nfl/Tagliabue-decision-bounty-appeal.pdf (pg 22)

143. http://www.nfl.com/news/story/09000d5d8298de65/article/stephen-burbank-rejects-nflpas-bounty-grievance?module=HP11_breaking_news

144. http://content.usatoday.com/communities/thehuddle/post/2012/06/report-arbitrator-upholds-roger-goodells-ability-to-suspend-saints/1#.UQUlBh3O2Pp

145. http://www.nola.com/saints/index.ssf/2012/06/arbitrator_rules_against_new_o.html

146. http://www.nola.com/saints/index.ssf/2012/06/new_orleans_saints_linebacker_33.html#incart_flyout_sports

147. http://www.nola.com/saints/index.ssf/2012/06/new_orleans_saints_linebacker_33.html#incart_flyout_sports

148. http://seanpamphilon.com/2012/05/31/when-you-kill-the-head-the-body-doesnt-die/

149. https://images.nflplayers.com/mediaResources/files/NFLPA_Annotated_Exhibits.PDF

150. https://images.nflplayers.com/mediaResources/files/NFLPA_Annotated_Exhibits.PDF

151. https://images.nflplayers.com/mediaResources/files/League%20Exhibits%201-12.pdf (pg. 6)

152. http://www.scribd.com/doc/99232293/Vilma-Amended-Complaint-1 (pg. 16, #86-88)

153. https://images.nflplayers.com/mediaResources/files/League%20Exhibits%201-12.pdf (pg. 79)

154. http://www.nola.com/saints/index.ssf/2012/06/new_orleans_saints_linebacker_33.html#incart_flyout_sports

155. http://www.nola.com/saints/index.ssf/2012/06/attorney_for_the_new_orleans_s.html

156. http://espn.go.com/blog/nfcnorth/post/_/id/42956/nflpa-statement-shame-on-nfl-goodell

157. http://espn.go.com/nfl/story/_/id/8067010/nfl-hears-bounty-appeals-players-cry-foul

158. http://espn.go.com/nfl/story/_/id/8067010/nfl-hears-bounty-appeals-players-cry-foul

159. http://espn.go.com/nfl/story/_/id/8067010/nfl-hears-bounty-appeals-players-cry-foul

160. http://espn.go.com/nfl/story/_/id/8067010/nfl-hears-bounty-appeals-players-cry-foul

161. http://www.nola.com/saints/index.ssf/2012/06/attorney_for_the_new_orleans_s.html

162. http://profootballtalk.nbcsports.com/2012/06/18/explosive-compelling-evidence-is-also-irrelevant-if-not-given-to-nflpa-on-friday/

163. https://www.nflplayers.com/Articles/Press-Releases/Outside-Counsels-Findings-on-Bounty-Investigation/

164. https://www.nflplayers.com/Articles/Press-Releases/Outside-Counsels-Findings-on-Bounty-Investigation/

165. https://www.nflplayers.com/Articles/Press-Releases/Outside-Counsels-Findings-on-Bounty-Investigation/

Chapter 13

166. http://sportsillustrated.cnn.com/2012/writers/dave_zirin/06/22/scott-fujita-bounty/

167. http://sportsillustrated.cnn.com/2012/writers/dave_zirin/06/22/scott-fujita-bounty/

168. http://sportsillustrated.cnn.com/2012/writers/dave_zirin/06/22/scott-fujita-bounty/

169. http://sportsillustrated.cnn.com/2012/writers/dave_zirin/06/22/scott-fujita-bounty/

170. http://www.scribd.com/doc/99232293/Vilma-Amended-Complaint-1 (pg. 25 #149 - 151)

171. http://www.scribd.com/doc/99232293/Vilma-Amended-Complaint-1 (pg.4, #19)

172. http://www.scribd.com/doc/99232293/Vilma-Amended-Complaint-1 (pg.4, #20)

173. http://www.scribd.com/doc/99232293/Vilma-Amended-Complaint-1 (pg. 22, #138)

174. http://profootballtalk.nbcsports.com/2012/07/02/vilma-suit-outs-mike-cerullo-as-bounty-whistleblower/

175. http://www.sportsnola.com/sports/saints/saints-news/583598-local-author-donnes-identifies-alleged-bounty-gate-whistle-blower.html

176. http://www.scribd.com/doc/99232293/Vilma-Amended-Complaint-1 (pg. 20, #119)

177. http://www.scribd.com/doc/99232293/Vilma-Amended-Complaint-1 (pg. 20, #118)

178. http://www.nola.com/saints/index.ssf/2013/01/joe_vitt_testimony.html

179. http://www.nola.com/saints/index.ssf/2013/01/joe_vitt_testimony.html

180. http://profootballtalk.nbcsports.com/2012/12/14/new-vilma-filing-targets-alleged-warner-bounty-cerullos-credibility/

181. http://profootballtalk.nbcsports.com/2012/12/14/new-vilma-filing-targets-alleged-warner-bounty-cerullos-credibility/

182. http://www.scribd.com/doc/99232293/Vilma-Amended-Complaint-1 (pg. 20, #120-121)

183. http://www.nola.com/saints/index.ssf/2013/01/joe_vitt_testimony.html

184. http://www.scribd.com/doc/99232293/Vilma-Amended-Complaint-1 (pg. 21, #122)

Chapter 14

185. http://www.scribd.com/doc/99232293/Vilma-Amended-Complaint-1 (pg. 21, #123, #125)

186. http://www.scribd.com/doc/99232293/Vilma-Amended-Complaint-1 (pg. 22, #137)

187. http://www.nfl.com/news/story/09000d5d82a4e6b7/article/player-discipline-for-saints-bounties-upheld-by-roger-goodell

188. https://www.nflplayers.com/Articles/Press-Releases/NFLPA-Statement-on-Commissioner-Goodells-Ruling/

189. http://www.freehgroup.com/leaders?leader=1#leader

190. http://www.freehgroup.com/

191. http://usatoday30.usatoday.com/news/nation/story/2012-07-12/louis-freeh-report-penn-state-jerry-sandusky/56181956/1

192. http://profootballtalk.nbcsports.com/2012/06/08/saints-hire-former-fbi-director-to-take-top-to-bottom-look-at-organization/

193. http://profootballtalk.nbcsports.com/2012/07/12/louis-freehs-next-task-investigating-the-saints/

194. http://sportsillustrated.cnn.com/college-football/news/20130128/mickey-loomis-saints-extension.ap/index.html

195. http://espn.go.com/nfl/story/_/id/8238319/sources-jonathan-vilma-suspension-reduced-withdraws-civil-suit

196. http://msn.foxsports.com/nfl/story/willie-roaf-hall-of-fame-snub-is-going-to-make-me-cry-020311

Chapter 15

197. http://espn.go.com/blog/nflnation/post/_/id/53386/what-theyre-saying-about-willie-roaf

198. http://www.nola.com/saints/index.ssf/2012/08/former_new_orleans_saints_ot_w.html

199. http://espn.go.com/nfl/story/_/id/8230985/new-orleans-saints-sean-payton-okd-attend-hall-fame-induction

200. http://www.wwltv.com/sports/black-and-gold/Sean-Payton-surprises-Saints-with-brief-visit-165035436.html

201. https://twitter.com/SportsLawGuy/status/228550373076512769

202. http://espn.go.com/nfl/story/_/id/8202975/new-orleans-saints-linebacker-jonathan-vilma-testifies

203. http://www.nola.com/saints/index.ssf/2013/01/joe_vitt_testimony.html

204. https://twitter.com/SportsLawGuy/status/228590521851998209

205. http://www.nola.com/saints/index.ssf/2012/08/roger_goodell_steadfastly_main.html

206. http://espn.go.com/nfl/story/_/id/8238319/sources-jonathan-vilma-suspension-reduced-withdraws-civil-suit

207. http://profootballtalk.nbcsports.com/2012/08/23/source-league-definitely-offered-eight-game-reduction-to-vilma/

208. http://www.grantland.com/blog/the-triangle/post/_/id/34543/who-dat-in-court-the-jonathan-vilma-case-explained

209. http://profootballtalk.nbcsports.com/2012/08/15/with-bounty-rulings-pending-judge-has-clear-concerns-about-process/

210. Vilma vs Goodell, August 10th court transcript (pg. 57)

211. Vilma vs Goodell, August 10th court transcript (pg. 70)

212. http://espn.go.com/nfl/story/_/id/8349080/suspensions-jonathan-vilma-smith-scott-fujita-anthony-hargrove-overturned-appeals-panel

213. NFLPA vs NFL, Summary Decision, In Matter of New Orleans Saints "Pay-for-Performance/Bounty" Program (pg. 3)

Chapter 16

214. NFLPA vs NFL, Summary Decision, In Matter of New Orleans Saints "Pay-for-Performance/Bounty" Program (pg. 4)

215. http://profootballtalk.nbcsports.com/2012/09/13/league-vilmas-lawyer-issue-new-statements-on-bounty-case/

216. http://profootballtalk.nbcsports.com/2012/09/13/league-vilmas-lawyer-issue-new-statements-on-bounty-case/

217. http://www.sportsonearth.com/article/38308546/

218. http://profootballtalk.nbcsports.com/2012/09/17/timing-of-gregg-williams-affidavit-raises-plenty-of-questions/

219. http://assets.espn.go.com/pdf/2012/0917/greggwilliamsdocument.pdf (#'s 2-4)

220. http://assets.espn.go.com/pdf/2012/0917/greggwilliamsdocument.pdf (#5)

221. http://assets.espn.go.com/pdf/2012/0917/greggwilliamsdocument.pdf (#11)

222. http://assets.espn.go.com/pdf/2012/0917/greggwilliamsdocument.pdf (#6-7)

223. http://assets.espn.go.com/pdf/2012/0917/greggwilliamsdocument.pdf (#7)

224. http://assets.espn.go.com/pdf/2012/0917/greggwilliamsdocument.pdf (#15)

225. http://www.youtube.com/watch?v=fhnn9kbqQUA (2:46 – 2:57)

226. http://assets.espn.go.com/pdf/2012/0917/greggwilliamsdocument.pdf (#12-13)

227. http://assets.espn.go.com/pdf/2012/0917/greggwilliamsdocument.pdf (#14)

228. http://www.nola.com/saints/index.ssf/2012/11/mike_cerullo_look_back.html

229. http://profootballtalk.nbcsports.com/2012/10/29/latest-vilma-brief-attaches-whistleblower-email-from-cerullo/

230. http://www.nola.com/saints/index.ssf/2012/03/full_nfl_statement_into_bounty.html

231. http://cbssports.com/images/blogs/cerullo_declaration09182012.pdf (#3)

232. http://cbssports.com/images/blogs/cerullo_declaration09182012.pdf (#5)

Chapter 17

233. http://profootballtalk.nbcsports.com/2012/12/14/new-vilma-filing-targets-alleged-warner-bounty-cerullos-credibility/

234. http://profootballtalk.nbcsports.com/2012/12/14/new-vilma-filing-targets-alleged-warner-bounty-cerullos-credibility/

Chapter 18

235. http://cbssports.com/images/blogs/cerullo_declaration09182012.pdf (#15)

236. http://cbssports.com/images/blogs/cerullo_declaration09182012.pdf (#16)

237. http://www.nola.com/saints/index.ssf/2013/01/joe_vitt_testimony.html

238. http://en.wikipedia.org/wiki/Bluegrass_Miracle

239. http://profootballtalk.nbcsports.com/2012/10/03/payton-loomis-vitt-will-attend-chargers-saints-game/

240. http://nfllabor.files.wordpress.com/2012/10/10-9-12-saints.pdf

241. http://www.nola.com/saints/index.ssf/2012/03/full_nfl_statement_into_bounty.html

242. http://www.nola.com/saints/index.ssf/2012/03/full_nfl_statement_into_bounty.html

243. http://nfllabor.files.wordpress.com/2012/10/10-9-12-saints.pdf

244. http://nfllabor.files.wordpress.com/2012/10/10-9-12-saints.pdf

245. http://nfllabor.files.wordpress.com/2012/10/10-9-12-saints.pdf

246. http://nfllabor.files.wordpress.com/2012/10/10-9-12-saints.pdf

247. http://espn.go.com/nfl/story/_/id/8484308/goodell-ruling-does-not-put-cap-saints-bounty-scandal

248. https://www.nflplayers.com/Articles/Press-Releases/NFLPA-Statement-on-Commissioner-Discipline/

249. http://profootballtalk.nbcsports.com/2012/10/09/jonathan-vilmas-statement-in-response-to-renewed-bounty-discipline/

250. http://profootballtalk.nbcsports.com/2012/10/11/brees-agrees-with-fujita-about-goodell-calls-bounty-case-a-sham/

251. http://www.whosay.com/AdamSchefter/content/413940?wsref=tw&code=iKk4lqC

252. http://nfllabor.files.wordpress.com/2012/10/10092012-memo-to-clubs.pdf (pg. 6)

Chapter 19

253. http://espn.go.com/nfl/playbyplay?gameId=291018018&period=0

254. http://nfllabor.files.wordpress.com/2012/10/10092012-memo-to-clubs.pdf (pg. 6)

255. http://espn.go.com/nfl/playbyplay?gameId=301107029&period=0

256. http://nfllabor.files.wordpress.com/2012/10/10092012-memo-to-clubs.pdf (pg. 4)

257. http://profootballtalk.nbcsports.com/2012/10/19/jimmy-kennedy-unloads-on-nfl-goodell/

258. http://profootballtalk.nbcsports.com/2012/10/19/goodell-recuses-himself-from-bounty-appeal/

259. http://espn.go.com/nfl/story/_/id/8524662/roger-goodell-hear-appeals-4-players-saints-bounty-case

260. http://espn.go.com/nfl/story/_/id/8524662/roger-goodell-hear-appeals-4-players-saints-bounty-case

261. http://www.neworleanssaints.com/news-and-events/article-1/Joe-Vitt-Discusses-Sundays-Loss-to-the-Denver-Broncos/ee384eb5-88a4-4a41-99f0-4091930ccb52

Chapter 20

n/a

Chapter 21

262. http://espn.go.com/nfl/story/_/id/8598047/sources-paul-tagliabue-recuse-self-arbitrating-bounty-appeals

263. http://espn.go.com/nfl/story/_/id/8592214/sean-payton-deal-new-orleans-saints-voided-nfl-sources-say

264. http://www.nola.com/saints/index.ssf/2011/09/new_orleans_saints_sign_contra.html

265. http://espn.go.com/nfl/story/_/id/8592214/sean-payton-deal-new-orleans-saints-voided-nfl-sources-say

266. http://espn.go.com/nfl/story/_/id/8592214/sean-payton-deal-new-orleans-saints-voided-nfl-sources-say

267. http://usatoday30.usatoday.com/sports/nfl/Tagliabue-decision-bounty-appeal.pdf

268. http://profootballtalk.nbcsports.com/2012/12/11/tagliabue-walks-tightrope-to-exonerate-players-goodell/

269. http://usatoday30.usatoday.com/sports/nfl/Tagliabue-decision-bounty-appeal.pdf (pg. 2)

270. http://usatoday30.usatoday.com/sports/nfl/Tagliabue-decision-bounty-appeal.pdf (pg. 4)

271. http://usatoday30.usatoday.com/sports/nfl/Tagliabue-decision-bounty-appeal.pdf (pg. 4)

272. http://usatoday30.usatoday.com/sports/nfl/Tagliabue-decision-bounty-appeal.pdf (pg. 6)

273. http://usatoday30.usatoday.com/sports/nfl/Tagliabue-decision-bounty-appeal.pdf (pg. 13)

274. http://usatoday30.usatoday.com/sports/nfl/Tagliabue-decision-bounty-appeal.pdf (pg. 17)

275. http://usatoday30.usatoday.com/sports/nfl/Tagliabue-decision-bounty-appeal.pdf (pg. 18)

276. http://usatoday30.usatoday.com/sports/nfl/Tagliabue-decision-bounty-appeal.pdf (pg. 18)

277. http://usatoday30.usatoday.com/sports/nfl/Tagliabue-decision-bounty-appeal.pdf (pg. 19)

278. http://usatoday30.usatoday.com/sports/nfl/Tagliabue-decision-bounty-appeal.pdf (pg. 19)

279. http://usatoday30.usatoday.com/sports/nfl/Tagliabue-decision-bounty-appeal.pdf (pg. 19)

280. http://usatoday30.usatoday.com/sports/nfl/Tagliabue-decision-bounty-appeal.pdf (pg. 20)

281. http://usatoday30.usatoday.com/sports/nfl/Tagliabue-decision-bounty-appeal.pdf (pg. 20)

282. http://usatoday30.usatoday.com/sports/nfl/Tagliabue-decision-bounty-appeal.pdf (pg. 20)

283. http://www.usatoday.com/story/sports/nfl/saints/2012/12/12/bounty-hearing-transcripts-gregg-williams-joe-vitt/1765241/

284. http://www.usatoday.com/story/sports/nfl/saints/2012/12/12/bounty-hearing-transcripts-gregg-williams-joe-vitt/1765241/

285. http://www.usatoday.com/story/sports/nfl/saints/2012/12/12/bounty-hearing-transcripts-gregg-williams-joe-vitt/1765241/

286. http://www.usatoday.com/story/sports/nfl/saints/2012/12/12/bounty-hearing-transcripts-gregg-williams-joe-vitt/1765241/

287. http://www.usatoday.com/story/sports/nfl/saints/2012/12/12/bounty-hearing-transcripts-gregg-williams-joe-vitt/1765241/

288. http://seanpamphilon.com/2012/05/31/when-you-kill-the-head-the-body-doesnt-die/

289. http://www.usatoday.com/story/sports/nfl/saints/2012/12/12/bounty-hearing-transcripts-gregg-williams-joe-vitt/1765241/

290. http://cbssports.com/images/blogs/cerullo_declaration09182012.pdf

291. http://www.usatoday.com/story/sports/nfl/saints/2012/12/12/bounty-hearing-transcripts-gregg-williams-joe-vitt/1765241/

292. http://profootballtalk.nbcsports.com/2012/12/14/new-vilma-filing-targets-alleged-warner-bounty-cerullos-credibility/

293. http://usatoday30.usatoday.com/sports/nfl/Tagliabue-decision-bounty-appeal.pdf (pg. 21)

294. http://usatoday30.usatoday.com/sports/nfl/Tagliabue-decision-bounty-appeal.pdf (pg. 19)

295. http://usatoday30.usatoday.com/sports/nfl/Tagliabue-decision-bounty-appeal.pdf (pg. 21-22)

296. http://usatoday30.usatoday.com/sports/nfl/Tagliabue-decision-bounty-appeal.pdf (pg. 22)

297. http://usatoday30.usatoday.com/sports/nfl/Tagliabue-decision-bounty-appeal.pdf (pg. 2)

298. http://usatoday30.usatoday.com/sports/nfl/Tagliabue-decision-bounty-appeal.pdf (pg. 3)

299. http://usatoday30.usatoday.com/sports/nfl/Tagliabue-decision-bounty-appeal.pdf (pg. 8)

300. http://usatoday30.usatoday.com/sports/nfl/Tagliabue-decision-bounty-appeal.pdf (pg. 3)

301. http://www.moosedenied.com/the-king-is-half-undressed/

302. http://usatoday30.usatoday.com/sports/nfl/Tagliabue-decision-bounty-appeal.pdf (pg. 16)

303. http://usatoday30.usatoday.com/sports/nfl/Tagliabue-decision-bounty-appeal.pdf (pg. 3)

304. http://usatoday30.usatoday.com/sports/nfl/Tagliabue-decision-bounty-appeal.pdf (pg. 8)

305. http://usatoday30.usatoday.com/sports/nfl/Tagliabue-decision-bounty-appeal.pdf (pg. 1)

306. http://usatoday30.usatoday.com/sports/nfl/Tagliabue-decision-bounty-appeal.pdf (pg. 6)

307. http://usatoday30.usatoday.com/sports/nfl/Tagliabue-decision-bounty-appeal.pdf (pg. 8)

308. http://usatoday30.usatoday.com/sports/nfl/Tagliabue-decision-bounty-appeal.pdf (pg. 14)

309. http://usatoday30.usatoday.com/sports/nfl/Tagliabue-decision-bounty-appeal.pdf (pg. 14)

310. http://usatoday30.usatoday.com/sports/nfl/Tagliabue-decision-bounty-appeal.pdf (pg. 14)

311. http://usatoday30.usatoday.com/sports/nfl/Tagliabue-decision-bounty-appeal.pdf (pg. 14)

312. http://usatoday30.usatoday.com/sports/nfl/Tagliabue-decision-bounty-appeal.pdf (pg. 17-18)

313. http://usatoday30.usatoday.com/sports/nfl/Tagliabue-decision-bounty-appeal.pdf (pg. 4)

314. http://usatoday30.usatoday.com/sports/nfl/Tagliabue-decision-bounty-appeal.pdf (pg. 15)

Chapter 22

315. http://www.nola.com/saints/index.ssf/2013/01/joe_vitt_testimony.html

316. http://usatoday30.usatoday.com/sports/nfl/Tagliabue-decision-bounty-appeal.pdf (pg. 7)

Legacy: Motives

317. http://usatoday30.usatoday.com/sports/nfl/Tagliabue-decision-bounty-appeal.pdf (pg. 1)

318. https://www.nflplayers.com/Articles/Press-Releases/NFLPA-Statement-on-Appeals-of-Discipline-Ruling/

319. http://www.nytimes.com/2012/12/23/sports/football/criticism-of-leadership-does-not-faze-nfl-commissioner-roger-goodell.html?pagewanted=all&_r=0

320. http://www.nola.com/saints/index.ssf/2013/01/joe_vitt_testimony.html

321. http://espn.go.com/nfl/story/_/id/8829996/sean-payton-new-orleans-saints-officially-signs-5-year-contract-extension

322. http://www.nola.com/saints/index.ssf/2013/01/judge_helen_berrigan_dismisses.html

Legacy: Credibility

323. http://sports.espn.go.com/nfl/news/story?id=1972285

324. http://sports.espn.go.com/nfl/news/story?id=1972288

325. http://sports.espn.go.com/nfl/news/story?id=1972288

326. http://sports.espn.go.com/chicago/nfl/news/story?id=6465271

327. http://www.nytimes.com/2013/01/11/sports/football/junior-seau-suffered-from-brain-disease.html?pagewanted=all

328. http://usafootball.com/#headsup

329. http://sports.espn.go.com/nfl/news/story?id=3244687

330. http://sports.espn.go.com/nfl/news/story?id=3244687

331. http://sports.espn.go.com/nfl/news/story?id=3244687

332. http://sports.espn.go.com/nfl/news/story?id=3244687

333. http://sports.espn.go.com/nfl/news/story?id=3244687

334. http://profootballtalk.nbcsports.com/2012/07/30/league-has-no-response-to-brees-criticism-of-goodell/

Legacy: Why Saints

335. http://www.nola.com/saints/index.ssf/2012/12/drew_brees_rips_into_roger_goo.html

336. http://espn.go.com/nfl/story/_/id/7881228/players-nfl-commissioner-roger-goodell-toughest-critics

337. http://espn.go.com/nfl/story/_/id/7881228/players-nfl-commissioner-roger-goodell-toughest-critics

338. http://www.usatoday.com/story/sports/nfl/2013/01/27/roger-goodell-nfl-players-approval-rating-super-bowl/1868953/

339. http://espn.go.com/espn/story/_/page/RogerGoodell/game-rules

340. http://www.usatoday.com/story/sports/nfl/2013/01/27/roger-goodell-nfl-players-approval-rating-super-bowl/1868953/

341. http://espn.go.com/blog/nfcsouth/post/_/id/10303/payton-reveals-super-details-in-book

342. *Home Team: Coaching the Saints and New Orleans Back to Life* (pg. 284 - 285)

343. http://profootballtalk.nbcsports.com/2010/05/01/sean-payton-implicated-in-alleged-vicodin-theft-at-saints-facility/

344. http://profootballtalk.nbcsports.com/2010/05/01/sean-payton-implicated-in-alleged-vicodin-theft-at-saints-facility/

345. http://profootballtalk.nbcsports.com/2010/05/01/former-saints-director-of-security-opened-negotiations-with-2-million-demand/

346. http://www.nola.com/saints/index.ssf/2010/05/new_orleans_saints_coach_sean_75.html

347. http://www.cbssports.com/nfl/blog/jason-la-canfora/20120908/saints-likely-facing-significant-civil-penalties-from-federal-vicodin-investigation

Legacy: Final Word

348. http://espn.go.com/espn/story/_/page/RogerGoodell/game-rules

349. http://www.nola.com/saints/index.ssf/2013/01/nflpa_executive_director_demau.html

Made in the USA
Coppell, TX
20 December 2021